THE
GOLF
POCKET BIBLE

THE
GOLF
POCKET BIBLE

JEREMY CARTWRIGHT

This edition first published in Great Britain 2010 by
Crimson Publishing, a division of Crimson Business Ltd
Westminster House
Kew Road
Richmond
Surrey
TW9 2ND

A catalogue record for this book is available from the British Library.

ISBN 978 1 907087 110

Printed and bound by Lego Print SpA, Trento

ACKNOWLEDGEMENTS

For Caroline

Thanks also to Ed, who lived up to his name.

CONTENTS

INTRODUCTION

Golf is the closest game to the game we call life. You get bad breaks from good shots; you get good breaks from bad shots – but you have to play the ball where it lies.
Bobby Jones

Do you know your birdie from your dog-leg? Have you ever wondered why golfers shout 'Fore'? Do you want to find out how to play the perfect bunker shot, or why golf got Mary Queen of Scots into trouble in 1567? Do you need some tips to improve your game – or are you wondering how to get started? Then *The Golf Pocket Bible* is for you.

Golf is a sport enjoyed by all ages across the world. From its humble origins in the Middle Ages to the worldwide professional tours we know today, the game has cast its fascinating and addictive spell over such diverse characters as presidents, astronauts and film stars – without ever losing sight of the principles of sportsmanship and etiquette which underpin it.

The benefits of playing golf are manifold, combining exercise with enjoyment as well as an excuse to get together with your friends. Golf is also a compelling spectator sport, as demonstrated not just by the lasting fame of stars like Jack Nicklaus and Tiger Woods, and of tournaments like the Open and the Ryder Cup, but also by the stunning beauty of the world's top courses.

The Golf Pocket Bible provides you with everything you need to graduate from novice enthusiast to golfing expert, from tips on your swing to a guide on the sport's history, geography, and how you can play on the best courses in the world. The book is both a reference guide to golf, from its origins to the best players, tournaments and courses, and a source of handy hints and tips on how you can get started playing golf and improving your own game.

THE FIRST FRONT NINE: HISTORY OF THE GAME

Golf has been played for centuries, and has developed into one of the richest histories in sport. The game is built on the strong foundations provided by its founding fathers, upholding ancient traditions of fair play, etiquette and deference to the rules. Modern golf combines these principles with the best in modern technology and global competition.

◉ FOUNDATIONS OF ◉ THE GAME

The spiritual home of the game of golf is St Andrews in Scotland. Local lore has it that 12th-century shepherds invented the game of golf on the land which was to become the famous Old Course (see page 48) by clubbing stones into rabbit holes with sticks. However, the real origins of golf may lie even further back in time. Like all true legends, golf has many other foundation stories which seem to transcend cultures:

- The Romans played a game called 'paganica', which involved hitting a leather ball stuffed with wool. However, the objective of this game is lost in the mists of time – some have even suggested it may be a nearer ancestor of hockey.

- The Chinese game 'chuiwan', translated as 'strike pellet', is recorded in a 13th-century history book as being played by Emperors.

- During King Edward III's reign in the 14th century, a popular game called 'cambuca' was played with a 'crooked club and ball'.

Little more is known about this game except its similarity to the French sport 'chambot'.

- The Scottish game is set apart from the others by one simple stipulation: that the ball must land in a hole.

ORIGIN OF THE WORD 'GOLF'

The origin of the word 'golf' is shrouded in mystery, with a number of different theories purporting to explain the meaning.

- The Dutch word 'kolf' or 'kolve' and the Old German 'kolbe' translate as 'a club', and this is believed to have been translated in Old Scots dialect as 'golve', 'gowl' and 'gouf'. However, there is no evidence connecting the original words with the game of golf.

- The first written evidence relating to the game of golf was in 1457, using the Old English word 'gowfe' (pronounced 'gouf').

- A rumour that the word was adopted as an acronym for 'Gentlemen Only: Ladies Forbidden' has no factual basis, even if this may be true at some clubs!

- The Loudoun Gowf Club retains the traditional spelling to this day.

Pocket Fact

In Scotland alone, documentary evidence exists of eight different spellings of the word we now know as 'golf': goff, gowf, golf, goif, gof, gowfe, gouff and golve!

Timeline of major events in the history of golf

- **1457:** King James of Scotland bans the sport of 'gowfe' because it was distracting too many Scotsmen from the archery practice necessary for defence of the realm. This decree is the first written mention of the game.

- **1553:** The land that will become the St Andrews course is given to the citizens of St Andrews for the playing of 'golff, futball, schuteing and all gamis'.

- **1567:** Mary Queen of Scots' enthusiasm for golf causes a scandal when she is seen playing at St Andrews within days of her husband's murder. She is the first known female golfer.

- **1744:** The first recorded rules of golf are written by the Gentlemen Golfers of Leith, and formalised 10 years later by the Royal and Ancient Golf Club of St Andrews (R&A).

- **1764:** The R&A reduces the number of holes on the golf course from 22 to 18.

- **1810:** Musselburgh Golf Club introduces a prize for 'the best female golfer'.

- **1860:** The first Open Championship is contested at Prestwick between eight of the finest professional golfers in England and Scotland. The first winner was Willie Park Sr.

- **1861:** The Open Championship is opened up to amateurs as well as professionals.

- **1873:** The Open is moved from Prestwick for the first time. From then on, the venue was rotated to a different course each year, a tradition that continues to this day.

- **1893:** The first Ladies' Championship is played.

- **1895:** The first US Open is played.

- **1916:** The US Professional Golfers' Association is founded, and the inaugural US PGA Championship played.

- **1927:** The first official Ryder Cup competition is played.

- **1934:** The first US Masters is played on the new course at Augusta.

- **1962:** Jack Nicklaus wins the first of his record 18 major championships.
- **1972:** The European Tour is formed.
- **1976:** The first British Women's Open is held.
- **1986:** Jack Nicklaus wins his final major at the age of 46.
- **2000:** Tiger Woods becomes the youngest player to win all four major tournaments.
- **2016:** Golf is readmitted as an Olympic sport.

Pocket Fact

The first golf club (and tournament) was established in 1744, when a group of players who practised on Leith Links petitioned the city of Edinburgh to provide a prize for the winner of an open competition.

Golf at the Olympic Games

Despite its worldwide popularity, golf has not been an Olympic sport since 1904. However, this will change in 2016 when the sport is welcomed back into the Games at Rio de Janeiro, along with rugby sevens.

What happened the last time golf was played at the Olympics?

The 1904 Games, held in St Louis, featured two golf competitions:

- *Men's singles. George Lyon of Canada won the gold medal, with United States golfers taking silver and bronze.*
- *Men's teams. Teams representing the United States won all three medals.*

How will golf at the 2016 Olympics be different?

- *There will be one men's-singles and one women's-singles competition, with no team event.*

- *The tournaments will be in stroke-play format rather than the match play of 1904. (See page 22 for an explanation of these formats.)*
- *The International Golf Federation has recommended that both tournaments have a field of 60 players, with the top-15 players in the world qualifying automatically.*
- *Outside the top 15, there is a suggested maximum of two players per country, to prevent individual countries dominating the competition.*

Pocket Fact

The first American woman to win an Olympic gold medal was a golfer. Chicago socialite Margaret Abbott won the only women's golf event at the 1900 Paris Olympics.

WHAT WAS AN EARLY GAME OF GOLF LIKE?

Although modern golf has retained many of the traditions of its past, a game of golf in the early days of the Open would have looked and felt very different from how it does now.

Players

Early amateur golfers were overwhelmingly from the upper classes, and would dress as such, even when out on the course (see page 7).

Golf balls

The first golf balls were fashioned from wood, until the development of a more sophisticated technique in the 17th century. The 'featherie' ball consisted of goose feathers packed into a leather sphere, and this remained the norm until the invention of the Gutta Percha ball in 1848. The Gutta was derived from the sap of a tropical tree, and its introduction made golf balls much cheaper to produce. The original design included a smooth surface, but golfers soon realised that it flew further after a few rounds, when nicks started to appear on the surface. Over the years this dimpled appearance became part of the standard design, with technological advances enabling a harder outer shell that allowed the ball to travel even further. More recently, the benefits of space-age plastics and silicone have also been utilised for further improvement.

Pocket Fact 🚩

Enough feathers were crammed into 19th-century golf balls to fill a top hat!

Golf clubs

Like modern players, early golfers used a number of clubs of different shaft lengths and club-face lofts, with Scotland renowned for its club-making expertise. However, the materials used were very different: shafts and club-heads were usually made with different kinds of wood, and iron clubs were hand-forged, unwieldy, and used only in the most desperate circumstances. With the appearance of the more resilient Gutta Percha ball, iron clubs could be used more frequently, and golf clubs began to move away from the old spoon-like style into more defined and sophisticated designs, with such exotic names as the 'mashie' and the 'niblick'. Most clubs continued to be handmade from wood until the early 20th century, with steel shafts only accepted by the golf authorities in the 1920s. By the 1980s, 'woods' (see page 25) were wooden in name only, as the wooden club-heads had also been replaced by metal.

Pocket Fact 🚩

The first known club-maker was William Mayne, who was appointed club-maker to the court of King James I in 1603.

Course

The first golf courses were developed on 'links' land (see page 42), because of this terrain's lack of suitability for farming. Lack of earth-moving equipment meant that the course was naturally sculpted from the land itself.

Other accessories

The first golfers were relatively low-maintenance compared to modern players: they needed little other than a bag to carry their clubs in.

Pocket Fact

Golfers have always tried to improve equipment: a recent auction in north-west England included a 19th-century practice golf ball attached by string to a parachute, so the golfer would not have to walk as far to retrieve it!

FASHION IN GOLF

'Play it as it lies' is one of the fundamental dictates of golf.
The other is: 'Wear it if it clashes'.
Henry Beard

While 'golf fashion' may sound like a contradiction in terms, the sport has gained a reputation as an opportunity for outrageous fashion statements. Golf fashion has evolved considerably through the ages:

- **Pre-1700**. The Scottish shepherds who first played the sport in Scotland would most likely have worn a purely functional ensemble of kilts and animal skins.

- **1700–1900**. Costumes increasingly reflected the fashions sported by the European nobles who most frequently played the game: knee-length breeches, tailcoats, and ruffled cravats.

- **1900–1925**. Longer trousers became the clothing of choice at all levels of society, reflected in golfing circles by the advent of 'plus fours' or 'knickerbockers' – longer trousers tucked into long socks. The rest of the outfit remained stiflingly formal, with long-sleeved button-ups, ties and newsboy caps the order of the day.

- **1925–1950**. In keeping with wider trends, golfing apparel became less formal – the dashing golfer-about-town might now be seen without a formal jacket, although ties were retained along with the practice of tucking trousers into long socks. In the absence of a jacket, the V-neck sweater gained popularity on chilly days.

- **1950–present**. Golfers began to move towards the casual dress code of the smarter elements of contemporary society: sweaters, polo shirts and slacks – not all colour-co-ordinated. As the 20th century neared its end, sponsorship started to encroach into golf-clothing design, with Tiger Woods, decked head to toe in Nike, leading the sober procession of polo shirts and baseball caps. However, outlandish golf fashion is on the way back, as a new generation, led by the English golfer, Ian Poulter (speciality: tartan trousers with Union-Jack waistcoat), compete to outdo each other on the fashion front.

EARLY PLAYERS

Due to golf's Scottish origins, the best players in the first years of competition were Scotsmen. The following trio won 11 of the first 12 Open Championships:

- **Willie Park Sr** won the first-ever Open at Prestwick in 1860. He went on to win four Opens in total.

- **Old Tom Morris** won the second and third Opens. A true golfing legend, he also won the Open four times, and was influential in early golf-course design (see Chapter 4), including his creation of the original Open course at Prestwick.

- **Young Tom Morris**, Old Tom's son, achieved the feat of winning the Open three years in succession, allowing him to keep the Championship belt permanently. Young Tom died at the age of just 24, having already won four Opens.

◎ GOLF'S POPULARITY ◎ INCREASES

Over the late 19th and early 20th century, golf became accessible to a wider section of the population, due to two major factors:

- **Mass production**. Golf balls were becoming increasingly cheap to buy, due to cheaper materials and production techniques. From the 1890s, golf clubs were also becoming cheaper due to the prevalence of steel shafts.

- **Affordability of travel**. Owing to the expanding network of railways, including a branch to St Andrews itself (although this station no longer exists), more and more people were able to travel to distant areas in their leisure time, leading to a dramatic increase in the number of golf clubs in the countryside.

TURNING PROFESSIONAL

Professional golfers have existed since the beginning of competitive golf – the first Open invitation was only extended to professionals. However, the prize money offered by these competitions did not provide golfers with sufficient income to live on until well after the formation of the first Professional Golfers' Association (PGA) in 1901, and many clubs still refused entry to professionals as late as the 1920s. The standard-bearer for early professional golfers was Walter Hagen, who raised the profile of professionals through his flamboyant showmanship both on and off the course. By the end of his career, Hagen had become possibly the first sportsman to earn $1m (approx. £700,000), and he transformed attitudes to professional golfers for good.

Pocket Fact ⛳

At the 1920 Open Championship, Walter Hagen used his chauffeur-driven limousine as a changing room, in protest at professionals not being allowed to use the front door of the clubhouse.

Development of tours

Originally, each professional golf tournament was established by an individual golf club. As professional golfers began to play more tournaments, these began to be organised into 'tours' organised by a single body. The first tour to be established was the PGA Tour in the USA, which had its origins in the foundation of the PGA of America in 1916, although the Tour itself was not officially established until 1968. By this time, the Ladies' Professional Golf Association Tour (LPGA) had also come into existence in 1950, and the PGA European Tour, the second-largest tour in professional golf behind the US PGA Tour, was established in 1972. Today, the tours provide the structure of the professional golf season.

Pocket Fact

The total prize money offered by the PGA Tour was $275m (approx. £190m) in 2009.

◉ DIFFERENT TYPES OF GOLF ◉

While playing on a full-size course remains the most popular form of golf, various offshoots of the sport have developed over time.

Pitch and putt

So named because you only need a pitching wedge and a putter to play, pitch and putt has a drastically shortened fairway, allowing players to pitch straight onto the miniature green.

What's good about it? You can find pitch and putt courses in public parks, as they don't take up as much space as the full-size version. A round (most are nine holes long) is relatively cheap.

What's bad about it? There is less interest for the serious golfer, as the shots require little strategic thought.

Crazy golf (US: mini golf)

A popular fixture at UK seaside resorts, this version of the game comprises very short holes on tarmac or AstroTurf instead of grass, with a variety of zany man-made obstacles between the tee and the hole (think windmills, bridges and X-shapes).

What's good about it? It's fun for all the family – the holes are only a few metres long so anyone can play. Entry is cheap, and kids love it.

What's bad about it? It is a game of luck rather than skill. Scores can sometimes be higher on these seemingly simple holes than on a full-length par 5: there's every chance your ball may roll or rebound all the way back to your feet!

Golf museums around the world

If you want to learn more about the history of golf, there is a select group of eminent museums around the world dedicated to just that.

The United States Golf Association (USGA) Museum

The most celebrated golf museum in the world. Based in New Jersey, it contains the world's largest collection of golf artefacts, which has so far taken 74 years to amass.

- *Key exhibits include Francis Ouimet's scorecard from the 1913 US Open, the only golf club used on the moon, and President Eisenhower's golf equipment.*
- *The museum is open from Tuesday to Sunday every week.*

The British Golf Museum

This is situated opposite the R&A Golf Clubhouse near to the Old Course at St Andrews. Housing the largest public collection of golf memorabilia in Europe, the museum opened in 1990.

- *Key exhibits include the oldest-known set of golf clubs in the world, and minutes from the earliest meetings of the R&A.*
- *The museum is open to the public every day.*

The European Golf Museum

Located in the German city of Regensburg, golf historian, Peter Insam, founded the museum in 1996 to house his collection of golf memorabilia and antiques.

- *Key exhibits include metal club-heads over four centuries old, and King George V's scorecard dating from 1922. (He shot 117.)*
- *The museum is open from Monday to Saturday every week.*

2

FROM ALBATROSS TO WATER HAZARD: THE RULES OF GOLF

The Game of Golf consists of playing a ball with a club from the teeing ground into the hole by a stroke or successive strokes in accordance with the Rules.
Rule 1.1, R&A Rules of Golf

Golf can seem a daunting game to approach for a beginner, and even seasoned players can sometimes be stumped by the rules. Here is a brief rundown of the essential parts of the game of golf, and the basic rules you need to know.

◎ PLAYING A HOLE ◎

- Place your ball on the tee (a short peg pressed into the ground, which positions the ball in mid-air to enable a lofted first shot).

- Measure the distance you need to drive (hit) the ball from the tee towards the hole (see page 147 for tips on how to measure distance).

- Select the right club, depending on the distance and type of shot required (see page 25 for a guide to different clubs).

- Drive the ball down the course, towards the hole.

- Locate your ball on the course, and take as many additional strokes as required to get your ball on the green (the area of short grass which surrounds the hole).

- Once your ball is on the green, take as many putts (strokes) as required until you hit it into the hole.

- Repeat on the next 17 holes to complete the course. Sounds simple, doesn't it?

Pocket Fact 🏌

The longest drive recorded in a golf tournament was 515 yards: the length of five football pitches!

◉ ESSENTIAL PARTS OF A COURSE ◉

Teeing ground

Usually known as the 'tee', this is the starting point of each hole, from which all players must take their first shot. The tee is signified by a pair of markers, laid up to six paces apart. As well as showing you where to start from, the markers are positioned to help guide your shot from the tee: if you are facing the hole, the markers will be either side of you. Most courses have at least three separate sets of differently coloured tee markers, which denote different yardages (and therefore difficulty) for the hole:

- **Championship tee (usually coloured blue or white)**. The furthest markers from the hole, used by male golfers with low handicaps or for championship play.

- **Men's tee (yellow)**. The next tee marker towards the hole, used most often by men with mid-range or high handicaps.

- **Ladies' tee (red)**. Located in front of the men's tee and most commonly used by women.

- **Juniors' tee**. The teeing area for juniors or beginners, not present on all courses.

Fairway

This is the strip of short grass between the tee and the putting green, where the ball will land if your drive is straight from off the tee. Landing on the fairway gives you a better 'lie' (how the ball sits on the ground) and a central position from which to play towards the hole.

Rough

The longer grass along each side of the fairway, where you may end up if your drive is off-course to either side. This gives you a trickier follow-up shot, as you are likely to have more difficulty making clean contact with the ball.

Out of bounds

If your ball flies beyond the designated boundaries of the course, it is judged to be out of bounds, which means you must play again from your original position, and incur an additional one-stroke penalty. If you think your ball is out of bounds, you should play a 'provisional ball' before searching for it – this means that if the original ball is lost you can continue play more quickly.

Bunker

A shaped crater, usually filled with sand. Bunkers are positioned near the green or on the fairway, to trap off-course balls and disadvantage the player for their next shot. Although the sand wedge (a tailor-made club with a lofted face) is available to help you get back on the straight and narrow, getting out of a bunker remains one of the most difficult skills in the game.

Water hazard

One thing I've learned over time is, if you hit a golf ball into water,
it won't float.
Arnold Palmer

Many courses are designed to be both scenic and deadly – especially those with water hazards like lakes or streams! If you hit your ball into the water, you have three options:

- Play the ball as it lies.

- Take a one-stroke penalty and play from where you hit the ball into the water.

- Take a one-stroke penalty and drop your ball onto the bank: you can drop the ball as far back as you like from the point of entry into the water, keeping your ball in line with the hole, or (in the case of a lateral water hazard running alongside the hole) within two clubs' length of the point of entry.

Putting green

The green is a well-maintained area of short grass surrounding the hole. If your ball is on the green, well done – you've negotiated all the hazards and are now within putting distance of the hole! But beware: while it looks flat at first glance, the green's carpet-like surface may conceal all kinds of hidden undulations. Make sure you take a good look at the ball's path to the hole before you line up your putt.

Hole

This is the target you need to aim the ball at. The hole's location on the putting green is signposted by a coloured flag, so that it can be seen from the fairway. The hole may be located anywhere on the green, and most courses change hole locations periodically. There are 18 holes on a full-size golf course, and a full circuit of all of them is known as a 'round'.

Pocket Fact ⚑

Until the early 20th century, golfers would make tees out of piles of sand. Original sand boxes can still be found at some old courses, although they now contain fertilised soil for filling in divots caused by errant club swings.

◉ THE BASIC RULES OF GOLF ◉

As we saw above, the objective of golf is to strike a small, hard ball from a set starting point into a hole using a variety of sticks known as 'golf clubs', in the fewest strokes possible. But just what rules do you have to follow to achieve this apparently simple objective?

ORIGINS OF THE RULES

The earliest surviving rules of golf were drawn up in 1744 by the Gentlemen Golfers of Leith (now the Honourable Company of Edinburgh Golfers), and adopted 10 years later by the St Andrews Golfers, who, in 1834, were renamed the Royal & Ancient Golf Club of St Andrews (now R&A) when King William IV agreed to become their patron. Together with the US Golf Association, the R&A continue to take responsibility for the maintenance of the rules of the game. While there are 33 rules in total covering every eventuality, the R&A also provide a 'Quick Guide to the Rules', intended to help players self-regulate in the simplest way possible.

KEY RULES TO BE AWARE OF

Before you start

- Read the local rules on the scorecard or the noticeboard of the clubhouse.

- Put an identification mark on your ball – if you can't identify it on the course, it is considered lost.

- Count your clubs (you are allowed up to 14).

Playing the ball

- Play the ball as it lies – no matter how badly! You are not allowed to move or press any obstacle or part of the course to improve your position. You are allowed to move loose impediments such as twigs, stones or detached leaves – however, if this causes your ball to move you incur a one-stroke penalty.

- Similarly, if you are in a bunker or water hazard, you are not allowed to touch the ground with your hand or club before hitting the ball.

- To play a stroke, you must swing the club to hit the ball – no pushing or scooping of the ball.

- If you play the wrong ball, you lose the hole in match play (see page 22) or incur a two-stroke penalty in stroke play (see page 22). If someone hits your ball in error or their ball hits yours, you can replace it with no penalty.

- If you are faced with 'movable obstructions' (artificial obstacles such as rakes or tin cans), you can move them without penalty. If you are hampered by an 'immovable obstruction' (an artificial condition such as a surfaced road) or an 'abnormal ground condition' (casual water, ground under repair or holes made by wildlife), you are allowed to lift the ball and drop it within one club's length of the 'nearest point of relief', which is the closest spot where you can play an unobstructed shot.

Dropping the ball

- In situations like the one above, or if you believe your ball is unplayable, you may be required to drop the ball. When doing so, stand upright and drop the ball at shoulder height and arm's length.

On the green

- You can lift your ball off the green in order to clean it, as long as you mark the spot and replace it exactly where it laid. You can also repair ball marks or old hole plugs (previous hole locations on the green), but not any other damage.

- When playing a stroke on the green, make sure the flagpole is removed.

Etiquette

- Because golf is mostly played without a referee or umpire, the game relies on the integrity of the players. This is why etiquette is a fundamental part of the rules of the game – covering matters such as fairness, care of the course, safety, and consideration for other players.

- If you have inadvertently played a shot that is in danger of hitting someone, or if you cannot see where the ball is going, you should immediately shout a warning: traditionally 'Fore!'

- The importance of etiquette is reinforced on the back cover of the official rule book: 'Play the ball as it lies, play the course as you find it, and if you cannot do either, do what is fair.'

Pocket Fact

Although the warning 'fore' simply means 'watch out ahead' (like a ship's fore), it is reputed to originate from the 19th-century use of 'forecaddies', who were detailed to stand where the ball was likely to land to avoid the unnecessary expense of lost balls. The cry of 'fore' was to alert the forecaddie that the ball was on its way.

After you have finished playing

- In match play, ensure that the result of your match is posted.

- In stroke play, ensure that you complete your scorecard properly and hand it back in.

◉ PLAYING BY THE RULES ◉

Knowledge of the rules is critical at the highest level: the most innocuous breaches can trigger tough penalties. Golf etiquette demands that, even at the highest level of competition, players self-police and admit if they've made a mistake – a rarity in competitive sport. Here are some of the most famous rule infringements:

- **Rule 18–2b**: *'If a player's ball in play moves after he has addressed it (other than as a result of a stroke), the player is deemed to have moved the ball and incurs a penalty of one stroke.'* Bobby Jones was challenging for the 1925 US Open when, unbeknown to anyone around him, he saw his ball move very slightly as he shaped to hit a shot from the rough. Jones called a one-stroke penalty on himself, which ultimately cost him the championship: finishing level with Willie MacFarlane after 72 holes, he lost the play-off but gained a lasting reputation for sportsmanship.

- **Rule 6–6b**: *'After completion of the round, the competitor should check his score for each hole and . . . return [the scorecard] to the Committee as soon as possible.'* Roberto De Vincenzo, celebrating his 45th birthday, thought he was tied for the lead with Bob Goalby after the final round of the 1968 US Masters. Unfortunately, De Vincenzo had inadvertently signed for a four on the penultimate hole instead of the three strokes he took, handing the title to Goalby by one shot.

- **Rule 13–4b**: *'The player must not touch the ground in the hazard or water in the water hazard with his/her hand or a club.'* Playing in the 2006 Women's British Open, Michelle Wie was penalised two strokes after her backswing in a bunker made contact with a piece of moss. Asked if she would familiarise herself more closely with the rules in future, Wie (then 16) famously replied, 'Well, it is not actually great reading material.'

- **Rule 13–4c**: *'The player must not touch or move a loose impediment lying in or touching the hazard.'* Brian Davis was on the first play-off hole with Jim Furyk for the 2010 Verizon Heritage championship when his backswing caught a loose reed, technically contravening this rule. No one but Davis noticed this, and his self-imposed penalty cost him the chance of nearly $400,000. Furyk said, 'I respect and admire what he did.'

- **Rule 5–1**: *'The ball the player plays must conform to the requirements specified . . . by the R&A.'* J. P. Hayes only realised after playing a PGA-Tour qualifying tournament that he had accidentally been using a prototype golf ball not approved by the USGA. Although no one would have known otherwise, he called from his hotel room to admit his error and was disqualified as a result. 'Everybody [on the PGA Tour] would have done the same thing,' he said afterwards.

Pocket Caddie

A sly pseudonym for the clubhouse bar, it is said that the '19th hole' is as much a part of the golfing experience as the first 18. Whether you are basking in the glory of a 'hole in one' (see page 22) or arguing over that missed putt on the last green, the 19th hole is the perfect place for convivial reflection at the end of a long and taxing round. If your chosen course does not have a clubhouse, fear not: the term can apply equally to a pub, bar or restaurant near the course.

All I've got against golf is that it takes you so far from the clubhouse.
Eric Linklater, Poet's Pub, 1929

◉ SCORING AND HANDICAPPING ◉

All men may be made equal but holes on a golf course certainly aren't. A rating system called 'par' is used to help you recognise the distance and difficulty of each hole, figure out your strategy, and measure your golfing prowess.

PAR

The number of strokes that a professional golfer is expected to take on a hole. Holes usually vary from three to five strokes for par, according to the length of the hole: as a general rule, the par is calculated as the number of strokes required to reach the green plus an expected two putts once on the green. Players taking fewer strokes than the designated par are said to be 'under par', whereas players taking more strokes are 'over par'.

Scoring against par

Golf is not just a numbers game; and in keeping with this ethos, names have developed for every conceivable score against par on a single hole (see the Glossary for more detail on the origins of each term).

- 4 under par (e.g. taking 1 stroke on a par 5 hole): Condor

- 3 under par: Albatross

- 2 under par: Eagle

- 1 under par: Birdie

- Level par: Par

- 1 over par: Bogey

- 2 over par: Double Bogey

- 3 over par: Triple Bogey
- 4 over par: Quadruple Bogey

HANDICAP

A handicap is a numerical measure of an amateur golfer's playing standard, representing the number of strokes above par that the player would achieve on an above-average day. While the primary purpose of the handicap system is to allow all players to compete on a fair and equal basis, regardless of ability, it is equally useful as a record of personal performance by which to measure your golfing progress over time.

◎ BASIC FORMS OF GOLF ◎

There are two principal methods of playing competitive golf: stroke play and match play.

STROKE PLAY

This is decided by the total number of strokes taken to complete the round against a field of competitors. Stroke play is generally considered to be the most demanding form of competition play, and is therefore the most common format of professional golf competition. In stroke-play competition at amateur level, your handicap is subtracted from your score at the end of the round.

MATCH PLAY

This is decided by the number of holes won and lost against a single opponent. At amateur level, match play tends to be the more common format. The handicap strokes are assigned by individual hole, due to the hole-by-hole nature of the match-play format.

Hole in one

The crowning glory for a golfer is a 'hole in one', where the ball lands in the hole straight from the tee shot. Holes in one are a rarity from the humble amateur to the most talented professional:

the chances of hitting a hole in one have been calculated at roughly 1 in 12,750 – or, in other words, your 709th round! While you don't have to be a professional to hit a hole in one – luck often plays a part – professional golfers stand a considerably better chance, as this list of high achievers demonstrates:
- *Jack Nicklaus – 19*
- *Arnold Palmer – 19*
- *Gary Player – 18*
- *Tiger Woods – 18 (the first when he was just six years old!)*

Pocket Fact
Three US presidents, all Republicans, have recorded holes in one: Dwight Eisenhower, Richard Nixon and Gerald Ford.

HOW TO BECOME A GOLFER

WHERE TO PLAY

With over 2,100 golf courses in England alone, there is sure to be a course near you. A number of websites exist to help you find your nearest golf course, and most courses will also be listed in your telephone directory.

Public or municipal courses

You do not have to be a member of a club to play golf: most people start out by playing on public (also known as municipal) golf courses, where an 18-hole round can be booked for as little as £20, depending on the course. Although golf is sometimes portrayed as snobbish and exclusive, public courses generally have a more relaxed attitude and are suitable for all standards of golf.

Private clubs

More serious golfers are likely to graduate to private clubs – the fees are higher (the average joining fee is £738 for men and £686 for women) but this allows you unlimited access all year round, and a range of 'members only' benefits such as additional tee times, tournaments and other events. Not all clubs are easy to join, and you may be put on a waiting list. For the most popular courses you may even need to be recommended by an existing member. However, some clubs are relaxing their membership policies in the current economic climate, so it's worth checking on the latest situation.

Pay and play

If you are not ready to opt for full membership, some private clubs also offer 'pay and play' options, where you can play a round for a one-off fee, enabling you to access the benefits of membership without requiring the full-membership investment. 'Pay and play' is a good option if you can't afford full-membership fees, or if you don't want to commit to one single course.

GETTING A HANDICAP

A handicap is an important step towards improving your golf game, as it allows you to play against more experienced golfers. To get an official handicap under the CONGU (Council of National Golf Unions) Unified Handicapping System, you need to be a member of a golf club or society recognised by the local golf authority. Most clubs require you to be accompanied for three rounds by a golfer with an existing handicap, who can vouch for your true score. The detail of the rules may vary by individual club, so it's best to check with the club's handicap secretary for its precise requirements. If you are not a member of a golf club or society, or if you just want to keep track of your golfing prowess, there are a host of internet sites that provide a free and convenient way of tracking your own handicap.

WHO TO PLAY WITH

If you are a first-time golfer, it's a good idea to start off with someone who is a more experienced player than you. They will be able to give you advice on how to play each stroke, which clubs to use, and the rules of the game. Ideally they should be either a friend or a very patient soul, as you will probably take a lot longer than them to get round the course at first!

WHAT YOU WILL NEED

Golf clubs

While professional golfers carry a club for every conceivable situation, up to a maximum allowance of 14, be warned: purchasing an expensive set of clubs does not automatically improve your golfing prowess! Most golf shops offer a range of starter sets containing the basic range, but if you are initially just looking to 'test the water', it's best to look for a reasonably new second-hand set or borrow some clubs from a friend. Alternatively, many courses have clubs available for hire.

Types of clubs:

- **Woods**. So called because the rounded club-head was traditionally made of wood, these clubs hit the ball furthest, and are normally used for maximum distance from the tee – however, they should be used with caution as they are the least accurate of the club types. On longer holes, professional golfers will sometimes use 'fairway' woods for subsequent shots.

- **Irons**. Designed for greater accuracy, with a flat, angled face and a shorter shaft than a wood. Irons are normally used for approach shots to the green, or to loft over trees, rough or other hazards. A range of differently numbered irons is available: the number representing the loft of the club, with the least lofted clubs being the furthest hitters, but also the least accurate. The numbers range from the 1-iron (the least lofted at 16°) to the 9-iron (the most lofted at 41°).

- **Wedges**. Most commonly used for short, lofted shots around the green, but may also be necessary to play from the rough or a bunker elsewhere on the course. The most commonly used is the pitching wedge, although the full set of clubs includes three other types of wedge (sand, gap and lob) for different types of chipped shot.

- **Putter**. The most used club in golf, the putter performs the delicate task of rolling the ball into the hole over the short grass of the green. The old golf saying, 'Drive for show, putt for dough', still holds true today: there are more varieties of putter on the market than any other club, due to the importance of choosing the right putter.

Pocket Fact 🚩

While the putter may appear to strike the ball flat, the club-face actually has a slight loft, which prevents the ball from rebounding if it has made an indentation on the green.

Slow and steady wins the race

The most practical club-selection strategy for beginners prioritises accuracy over distance, as the longer clubs require a more proficient swing. An average starter set usually comprises the following: a range of two or three higher (more lofted) irons; pitching wedge; and a putter. Some starter sets replace one of the irons with a driver – you may want to have this in your repertoire if you feel confident about your swing. But if you decide to err on the side of caution, you are in good company: Jack Nicklaus won the 1966 British Open by mostly driving with a 1-iron for greater accuracy at the expense of power, in order to avoid the perilous rough.

Other essential equipment

There is a wide range of other equipment you can buy to help you play golf. If you do not own everything, many of these things can be hired at the club shop.

- **Shoes**. These have removable spikes on the sole, which provide extra traction when you are swinging the club in wet or slippery conditions. Golf shoes are usually mandatory: even if they are not, make sure that the shoes you wear have the most 'gripping' soles possible.

- **Bags**. A golf bag is essential for carrying your clubs round the course; modern bags also have many and varied pockets to carry your golf balls, towels, spare tees, umbrella and whatever else you are kitted out with. The more clubs you are carrying, the larger your bag needs to be — so if you are just starting out, a smaller size (known as a carry bag) will probably be the most practical. If you are planning on buying a golf trolley (see page 28) you may prefer to choose a 'trolley bag', which is tailor-made to fit into all types of trolley or cart.

Pocket Caddie

Don't choose your bag until you know exactly how much equipment you need it to carry!

- **Balls**. Golf-ball design has come a long way from the 16th century, when balls were fashioned from wood (see page 5). Today, the golf ball is one of the most highly engineered balls in the sports world — if you are a beginner, it is safest to start with the cheaper 'two piece' (a double-layered rather than multi-layered design) until you are familiar enough with your own game to decide what type of ball will work best for you.

- **Clothing**. While many courses have a specific dress code, private clubs are often stricter in this area than public clubs: if in doubt, check before you go to avoid an enforced pre-round visit to the club shop! Most clubs have a no-denim policy, even in the clubhouse; casual attire such as collarless shirts, open shoes, or replica football or rugby kit is also inappropriate. The safest option is a collared polo shirt, and non-denim trousers or Dockers-style shorts.

- **Gloves**. These increase your purchase on the club handle, which can be invaluable in wet or sticky weather.

- **Umbrellas**. As the average day in the great British outdoors has a 40% chance of rain, an umbrella is a valuable addition to your repertoire of accessories. A proper golf umbrella (larger than those you would see on the high street) is recommended rather than a tiny handbag-size one — it has to be big enough to cover both you and your golf bag. Golf umbrellas are also made to be highly wind-resistant, as strong winds can be a feature of many golf courses, particularly in the UK.

- **Waterproofs**. Sometimes it may be too windy even for an umbrella – in which case waterproofs are the last resort for the hardy golfer.

- **Tees**. It is possible to buy either wooden or plastic tees, depending on your preference: wood is the traditional material and used by the majority of professional golfers, while plastic tees are cheaper but can bend over time. Tees are a lower-risk purchase than other equipment, as they are relatively cheap and you can buy them in bulk. Tees come in a wide variety of colours, with white being the most popular.

Pocket Caddie

Avoid using green tees as they can easily get lost on the course.

- **Towels**. It is important to keep your clubs dry in wet weather, to make sure they do not slip out of your grasp and to enhance the control you can apply on the ball. Bespoke golf towels are available, but a household hand-towel will suffice if you don't want to spend additional money.

- **Trolleys**. If you're older, have a bad back, or would simply rather save energy for your swing than for dragging your clubs around, golf trolleys are on hand to ease your progress round the course. The modern golf trolley is made of light metal with a platform for your bag, and wheels which enable it to be pulled around easily. You can avoid even this exertion with an electric trolley which propels itself along using a motor and a battery – all you need to do is guide it.

Weird and wonderful golfing accessories

Since golf is a game where the equipment can make a real difference, there is a plethora of outlandish accessories which claim to improve your game. Some of them may — there's only one way to find out!

- **Robotic golf trolley.** The worlds of golf and artificial intelligence have collided with the invention of an electronic golf trolley that follows you automatically round the course. Simply clip a transmitter to your trousers or top, turn it on, and tee off. The trolley is smart enough to avoid hazards in its path — all you need to do is set it to 'follow' or 'stop'. However, it probably won't warn you to use your 1-iron instead of the driver . . .

- **Golf-ball monogram marker.** It is vital to know which golf ball is yours, as hitting the wrong one incurs a penalty — but what if your playing partner uses a similar ball to yours, or if you find more balls than you anticipated in the rough? Luckily, special stamps are available for you to personalise yours golf balls in a variety of colours with up to four letters — ideal for initials or a nickname.

- **Long-handled golf-ball retriever.** Fed up with losing your precious monogrammed balls in that lake at the 17th? A surprising variety of long-handled tools exist to help you retrieve your stranded ball — the key differences being how long you need the handle to be and whether you prefer a 'rake' or a 'grab' on the end of the handle.

- **GPS for golfers.** Not as in satellite-navigation systems — the tee markers tell you which direction to play in — but to keep you informed of exact distance to the hole from any angle of approach. These gadgets come with golf-cart mounts and belt clips to make it easy for you to carry round the course.

- **Indoor golf equipment.** If you can't always get to the course, all is not lost: you can kit your home out as well!

○ **Practice balls**. *Specially designed golf balls which feel just like the real thing, enabling you to practise your pitch and chip shots indoors without damaging windows or walls as outdoor golf balls would.*

○ **Putting machines**. *Famous for providing executive stress relief in boardrooms throughout the world, indoor putting machines have moved into the modern age with electronic enhancements. Where once there was just a ball and a cup, the indoor golfer can now putt on synthetic putting greens complete with real holes and bunkers, or putting machines that return the ball to your feet.*

○ **Swing monitors**. *Various devices are available to show you how your swing is working without needing to leave the house. Basic 'swing groovers' (usually a ball hanging free from a metal post) enable you to practice hitting the ball. More advanced electronic versions show you how to hit it better; most look like clubs but contain small devices that measure the angle, speed and direction of your swing, then tell you how you can improve. If you want to see the evidence with your own eyes, you can use a laser tracker which highlights the path of your swing.*

GET READY TO PLAY!

Do you have the following?

- Clubs

- Balls

- Tees

- Correct dress and shoes

- The rest of your golfing equipment (don't forget that electric trolley!)

Do you know

- Where you're playing
- Who you're playing with
- What time you're teeing off

Go play golf. Go to the golf course. Hit the ball. Find the ball, repeat until the ball is in the hole. Have fun. The end.

Chuck Hogan

3

THE CADDIE: A GOLFER'S BEST FRIEND (OR WORST ENEMY)

Wherever there is golf, there will always be caddies – whether just to carry the clubs or to advise on the right strategy and club selection. Here we take a look at the golfer's most indispensable companion . . .

◉ HISTORY OF THE CADDIE ◉

ORIGIN OF THE WORD

The word 'caddie' originates from the French word 'cadet', or 'youngest of the family', and first appeared in English in the 1630s. Mary Queen of Scots herself was reputedly responsible for its introduction into the golfing lexicon, having played golf during her years in France (where military cadets carried her clubs) and then upon her return to Scotland. Caddies were not just required to carry the clubs, but also to make a way through other activities taking place on the course, and to keep track of the ball.

Pocket Fact
The first recorded caddie was Andrew Dickson, who caddied for the Duke of York on Leith Links, in the first 'international' golf match between Scotland and England in 1682.

HOW THE ROLE DEVELOPED

As golf gained popularity over the 19th century, the role of the caddie ceased to be merely about carrying the baggage of the rich

and privileged, and began to develop into a more instructive relationship with the often inexperienced golfers playing the game.
Today, professional golfers depend on their caddies for support,
guidance and advice as they negotiate the course.

FORECADDIES

The job of the forecaddie is to move ahead of the group, in order
to keep track of everyone's shots, and to direct players round the
course. You are most likely to find them at more expensive or elite
clubs. At professional tournaments, marshals or spotters are often
employed to find balls that stray into the rough and keep the
crowd off the course.

Pocket Fact

*One of the potential explanations for the cry 'Fore!' is that this was
originally meant to alert the forecaddie to an approaching ball.*

◉ WHAT THE CADDIE CAN ◉ DO FOR YOU

The caddie's role covers a variety of duties:

CLUB CARRIER

This is the original reason for the presence of caddies on the
course, although the prevalence of trolleys and carts on most
courses has made this service optional rather than essential.

COURSE EXPERT

More than just a club-carrier, a good caddie will have detailed
knowledge of the course you are playing on, enabling them to
advise you on any aspect of the round:

- **Distance to the hole**. Your caddie will know each hole well
  enough to be able to accurately judge the distance to it, no
  matter where you are on the course.

- **Choice of club**. This depends not only upon the distance to the hole but also upon the type of shot required – are you better off launching it high into the air or driving it in low? What are the pitfalls and hazards you need to avoid?

- **Reading the green**. Greens often have subtle contours and undulations, which means the ball will rarely travel in a straight line to the hole. Caddies, who know the greens inside out, will be able to help you strike it in the right direction.

RESIDENT WIT

The caddie traditionally injects a slice of humour into proceedings, usually at their player's expense. As well as enlivening the round, a caddie's ready wit also has a psychological benefit as it deflates any pressure and keeps the mood upbeat.

CARETAKER

The caddie will clean your golf ball, and attend the flag when you are putting. The caddie also covers course upkeep on the way round – for example, raking over the sand in bunkers and replacing divots on the fairway.

CROWD CONTROLLER

At tournaments, the caddie also helps with crowd control – for example, protecting the golfer from flash photography.

◎ HOW YOU GET A CADDIE ◎

IN THE UK

In the UK, caddies are most likely to be available at the more exclusive private courses. One exception to this is St Andrews, which is one of the most notable public courses (see page 23). For most amateur golfers, playing with a caddie is a very rare treat but well worth investing in, particularly if you are playing on an unfamiliar course. If you are trying to arrange a caddie, contact the club in advance to find out whether this is possible.

FURTHER AFIELD

Caddies tend to be more common at the biggest and best courses in America and other golf hot spots like South Africa. Contact the club in advance to make arrangements.

◉ HOW MUCH DOES A CADDIE COST? ◉

CADDIE FEES

Caddie fees vary widely depending on the type of club, with fees at the most famous Scottish clubs like St Andrews reaching £40 plus tip. However, the fee is likely to be cheaper at less revered clubs. Contact the club professional or caddie master to find out how (and how much) to pay.

TIPPING

Attitudes to tipping can vary by golf course: at some, tipping is expected; at others, it may be discouraged or even prohibited. It's a good idea to ask ahead if you're unsure. Courses unlikely to encourage tipping include public (municipal) courses, or courses without a dress code. At the other end of the scale, the most exclusive American courses like Pine Valley or Augusta National (see Chapter 4) strictly forbid tipping in favour of a flat fee.

At courses where tipping is the norm, it will be expected that you tip the caddie on top of the standard caddie fee. If there's a caddie master – the person who assigns caddies to golfers or groups – you may be able to ensure a good caddie by tipping the caddie master.

The size of the tip is dependent on a number of factors:

- The quality of service you've been given by the caddie.

- Course knowledge such as distances, and quality of advice such as club choice and green reading.

- The cost of the golf club – the more expensive or prestigious the establishment, the higher the tip is expected to be.

Pocket Fact Ⓣ

The first electric golf carts appeared in the 1940s, marking a decline in reliance on caddies at some golf courses.

Caddie wit and wisdom

Caddies are legendary for their dry wit in the face of sometimes trying circumstances. Here are a few examples of the craft:

Golfer: I'd move heaven and earth to break 100 on this course.
Caddie: Try heaven: you've already moved most of the earth.

Golfer: Do you think I can get there with a 5-iron?
Caddie: Eventually.

Golfer: You've got to be the worst caddie in the world.
Caddie: I don't think so, sir. That would be too much of a coincidence.

Golfer: How do you like my game?
Caddie: Very good, sir, but personally, I prefer golf.

Golfer (after hooking his third tee shot in a row): Give me a club — I want to break something.
Caddie: How about 'par'?

Pocket Fact Ⓣ

Many of golf's legends — Gene Sarazen, Ben Hogan, Sam Snead, and Byron Nelson to name only a few — started out as caddies before becoming professional golfers.

◉ FAMOUS CADDIES ◉

Here are some of the most memorable caddies in the history of golf:

Francis Ouimet

A local boy who lived across the road from The Country Club in Brookline, Massachusetts, where he carried the bag for well-heeled members, Ouimet famously beat legendary professional golfers, Harry Vardon and Ted Ray, to win the 1913 US Open, aged just 20.

Fanny Sunesson

The first high-profile female caddie, Sunesson caddied for Nick Faldo from 1990 until 1999. She was later re-hired by Faldo and has also caddied for other top golfers including Sergio Garcia. Her advice for novice caddies is: 'Never be late, keep fit, always know your distances and make sure you know when to keep your mouth shut.'

Pocket Fact 🚩

Faldo and Sunesson married their respective partners on the same day in 2001.

Steve Williams

A no-nonsense New Zealander, Williams has caddied for Tiger Woods since 1999, having previously caddied for Ray Floyd and Greg Norman.

Jim 'Bones' Mackay

After starting out in 1990 with Larry Mize, Mackay was taken on by Phil Mickelson in 1992 and has been with him ever since, helping Mickelson to all four of his major championships.

Mike 'Fluff' Cowan

Famous for his luxuriant, white moustache, 'Fluff' caddied for Tiger Woods during his first two years as a professional, before being replaced by Steve Williams (see above). He was unemployed for only a few weeks before being snapped up by Jim Furyk, whom he helped to the US Open title in 2003.

Pocket Fact

When Steve Elkington won the 1995 US PGA Championship, he gave his winner's cheque to his caddie, Dave Renwick, as a 'thank you'.

◉ EVEN CADDIES GET IT WRONG ◉

Caddies have a thankless task, hitting the headlines only if they make mistakes – and in the cut-throat world of professional golf, a mistake by the caddie results in a penalty for their player. Here are some of the ways in which caddies have fallen foul of the complex rules of golf:

- Byron Nelson was winning the 1946 US Open at Canterbury – until his caddie accidentally kicked his ball, incurring a penalty stroke. Nelson ended up in a tie for the lead, and lost the 36-hole play-off.

- Ian Woosnam's caddie began the final round at the 2001 Open with 15 clubs in the bag – one more than the permitted 14 – that resulted in a two-shot penalty and cost the Welshman £218,334 in prize money.

- As Stuart Appleby took a free drop at the 2005 WGC-NEC Invitational, his caddie picked the ball up before it had rolled the required two clubs' length. The mistake cost Appleby over $A100,000 (approx. £57,500) . . . and the caddie his week's wages.

- David Merriman was bunkered at the 9th hole but tied for the lead in the 2007 Australian Senior Open, when his caddie – also his partner – raked the sand before he hit his shot. He incurred a two-stroke penalty . . . and finished one behind the winner.

Pocket Caddie

In the UK, there is a website for ordering attractive caddies who know the rules and etiquette of the game (www.eyecandycaddies. com) – a good idea for golfing boys' (or girls') holidays!

The R&A captain and the golden golf ball

The St Andrews caddies get more excited than most when the R&A install a new captain. Tradition dictates that the captain marks his appointment by driving a ball off the 1st tee at the Old Course to the blast of a cannon, and there is a race among the caddies to retrieve the ball. The winner is presented with a gold sovereign as a reward.

Six members of the royal family have been given the captaincy – most recently Prince Andrew who drove his tee shot 260 yards in 2003.

4

THE FINEST FAIRWAYS: GOLF'S FAMOUS COURSES

Unlike many sports, golf is defined by its surroundings: the nature of the terrain, the different hazards and obstacles, and even the elements themselves are integral to the playing experience. This chapter charts the finest examples of golf courses in the world, and the reasons why they are so revered.

◎ WHAT MAKES A GREAT ◎ GOLF COURSE?

A great golf course both frees and challenges a golfer's mind.
Tom Watson

There are nearly 32,000 golf courses in the world – but what makes one better than another? While there is no definitive course-ratings system, a number of features are generally held to be instrumental in 'grading' a course:

- **Design**. The overall structure of the holes: this can cover hole layout, difficulty, length, positioning and composition of hazards, the contouring of the fairways and greens, and pin positions.

- **Visual appeal**. This applies not just to the course itself but also to its surroundings. Spectacular scenery can dramatically enhance the beauty of a course – although as beauty is in the eye of the beholder, this can be a contentious subject!

- **Variation**. Does the course require a combination of skills (and therefore club selections) to play the best round? The great courses are 'challenging' as opposed to merely 'tough':

for example, it would be easy to design a course with narrow fairways, tiny greens and thick rough, but dull and predictable from a playing perspective.

- **Memorability**. Individual holes should live in the mind long after the round is finished.

- **Course condition**. Is the course well maintained? This covers both natural elements like fairways, rough and greens; and man-made additions like tee boxes, course perimeters, and the clubhouse.

- **Practice facilities**. The availability of a driving range, putting green, and practice bunkers.

◉ TOP COURSES BY REGION ◉

UK AND IRELAND

- Muirfield, Scotland
- Royal County Down (Championship Links), Northern Ireland
- Turnberry (Ailsa Course), Scotland
- St Andrews (Old Course), Scotland
- Royal Birkdale, England
- Ballybunion (Old Course), Ireland
- Carnoustie (Championship Course), Scotland
- Kingsbarns, Scotland
- Royal Portrush (Dunluce Links), Northern Ireland
- Royal Dornoch (Championship Course), Scotland

CONTINENTAL EUROPE

- Valderrama, Spain
- Les Bordes, France
- PGA Catalunya (Stadium Course), Spain

- Morfontaine, France
- Halmstad (North Course), Sweden

USA

- Pine Valley, New Jersey
- Cypress Point, California
- Augusta National, Georgia
- Pebble Beach Golf Links, California
- Shinnecock Hills, New York

REST OF THE WORLD

- Royal Melbourne (West Course), Australia
- Kingston Heath, Australia
- Cape Kidnappers, New Zealand
- Casa de Campo (Teeth of the Dog), Dominican Republic
- Leopard Creek, South Africa

Definition of a links course

The word 'links' is derived from the Anglo-Saxon 'hlinc', originally meaning a ridge but later applied to any coastal strip of land between the beach and inland, agricultural areas. Early golf courses were often located on this type of land as the sandy soil made it unsuitable for crops. Links courses came into being before the availability of earth-moving machinery and remain 'as nature intended', with relatively little course maintenance required. This is why most of the first golf courses were also links courses.

The defining characteristics of a traditional links course are:
- *Coastal location*
- *Windy climate due to sea breezes*
- *Sandy soil*

- *Open ground with few or no trees*
- *Natural course layout, including uneven fairways and thick rough*
- *Small bunkers known as 'pot bunkers'. These are very deep in order to prevent the sand being blown away by the wind.*

Pocket Fact

The Open Championship is always played on a links course.

◉ PROFILES OF FAMOUS COURSES ◉

UK

Muirfield

First played: 1891

Location: East Lothian, Scotland

History: Muirfield is home to The Honourable Company of Edinburgh Golfers, who drew up the original rules of golf in 1744. To this day, Muirfield retains a more formal air than most golf clubs. The course was designed by Old Tom Morris, and opened in 1891. Further enhancements were carried out between the wars by Harry Colt and Tom Simpson.

Pocket Fact

Greywalls Hotel, which has been an integral part of the Muirfield experience since 1928, has a secret back door connecting it to the course via the clubhouse.

Tournaments played there: 15 Open Championships, the Ryder Cup (1973), two Walker Cups, ten Amateur Championships.

Famous events:

- 1920: Cyril Tolley pays his caddie the money agreed for winning *before* holing the winning birdie putt in the Amateur Championship.

- 1959: Gary Player is left distraught after a double-bogey at the final hole convinces him he has lost the Open – but cheers up when the rest of the field fall back even further, leaving him victorious.

- 1972: Lee Trevino holes a chip from behind the 17th green to steal the Open from Tony Jacklin.

- 1987: Nick Faldo wins his first major championship, completing every hole of his final round in par.

Did you know? Muirfield has twice hosted the annual varsity match between Oxford and Cambridge universities – the only non-English venue to do so.

Course topography: Muirfield presents a subtle challenge: there are no trees or water hazards, and the course is not overly long by modern standards, but every hole is characterised by deep, hidden bunkers, tight fairways with thick rough, and small undulating greens. Muirfield was the first course to be structured in 'concentric nines' (two loops of nine holes, one inside the other), meaning that the wind direction is different on each successive hole.

Signature hole: 1st, 444 yards, par 4. The opening hole, described by Jack Nicklaus as one of the toughest in championship golf, is a sign of dangers to come: one of many large bunkers dominates the left of the narrow fairway, and severe rough lurks on the right, so an accurate drive is essential. The green slopes from front to back, so a high approach is the only option to avoid rolling off the back.

How do I get to play there? You can play the Muirfield course for green fees of £185 per round, if your handicap is no greater than 18 (for men) or 20 (for women). However, competition for places is fierce: tee times have to be booked months, sometimes years, in advance, so if you're planning a trip to Muirfield make sure you confirm your tee time first.

Pocket Caddie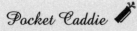

Book two rounds on the day for only £45 extra – after playing the course once, you will definitely want to go round again!

Royal County Down (Championship Links)

First played: 1889

Location: County Down, Northern Ireland

History: As with many golf courses of the late 19th century, the construction of the original course was connected with the development of a railway line, from Belfast to Newcastle. George L. Baillie, a Scottish schoolteacher, designed the first nine holes, and Old Tom Morris the second nine. The course was subsequently modified by George Combe, for which he was granted honorary life membership in 1909. Further enhancements since 1997 include a new 16th hole.

Tournaments played there: Walker Cup (2007), Curtis Cup (1968).

Did you know? The Mourne Mountains, which form the spectacular backdrop to the course, also inspired Belfast-born author, C.S. Lewis: he once told his brother that the landscape came closest to his idea of the magical land of Narnia, because 'at any moment a giant might raise his head over the next ridge'.

Course topography: Royal County Down winds alongside Dundrum Bay at the foot of the Mourne Mountains. The ribbon-like fairways cut through rugged dunes covered in purple heather and yellow gorse: a picturesque sight, but one to avoid if you want to find your ball! The 'bearded' bunkers, fringed with wild grasses, are a unique and dangerous feature. The greens are fast, domed and undulating, meaning putts need to be hit soundly to reach the hole.

Signature hole: 9th, 486 yards, par 4. One of the most spectacular holes in golf, the 9th was originally played as two holes. The view from the tee box, perched on a heather-strewn hill, is truly awe-inspiring, with the mountains in the distance and the bay to the left. But the tee shot has to clear a towering dune ridge to the fairway some 60 ft below, 260 yards from the tee. From the bottom of the slope the second shot is played over two bunkers to a raised green.

How do I get to play there? Visitors can play the course most days of the week – contact the secretary's office to confirm availability and make a booking. Green fees vary from £50 to £180 depending on the time of year. Due to the terrain, golf buggies are not permitted.

Pocket Fact

For his work designing the second nine holes, Old Tom Morris was paid the princely sum of 4 guineas: the equivalent of around £400 in today's money.

Turnberry (Ailsa Course)

First played: 1901

Location: Ayrshire, Scotland

History: Designed by Willie Fernie, Turnberry was opened in 1901 after the landowner, Lord Ailsa, combined the building of a golf course with the opening of a railway line from Ayr. The famous Station Hotel, which overlooks the course from the brow of a nearby hill, was opened in 1906 providing luxury unsurpassed at the time: a covered link-way connected the hotel with the railway station so guests would not arrive wet and bedraggled.

Pocket Fact

During the Second World War, the hotel was commissioned as a hospital, and the course was used as an RAF flying school.

Tournaments played there: Four Open Championships.

Famous events:

- 1977: The 'Duel in the Sun' (see page 133), after which the 18th hole has been renamed.

- 2009: Tom Watson, needing a par at the 18th to become the oldest winner of a major championship, drops a shot and is beaten in the play-off by Stewart Cink.

Did you know? Turnberry's iconic lighthouse was built by Thomas and David Stevenson, the father and uncle of the famous writer, Robert Louis Stevenson.

Course topography: Turnberry epitomises British links golf, with wrinkled fairways, deep bunkers, and wild rough running alongside breathtaking views over the Irish Sea – although, unlike most links courses, there are no dunes protecting the coastal holes. Bruce's Castle, the nearby 13th-century ruins belonging to Scottish king, Robert the Bruce, and the famous Turnberry lighthouse can both be seen in the middle of the round – seven consecutive holes are played alongside the ocean.

Signature hole: 9th, 449 yards, par 4. The tee is set on a rocky outcrop at the water's edge, and your ball must clear the corner of the bay to reach the 'blind' fairway. Although the hole has no bunkers, there are other dangers: a ridge in the middle of the fairway can send balls flying towards the rough, and the sloping green is protected by mounds and hollows.

How do I get to play there? Turnberry is open to the public, with green fees ranging from £90–£210 depending on the time of year. Despite the fame and stature of the course, it is usually possible to secure a midweek tee time.

Pocket Caddie

Make sure you book afternoon tea at the Turnberry Hotel after your round – it's delicious!

St Andrews (Old Course)

First played: 1553 (the date when locals were officially allowed to play golf on the links)

Location: St Andrews, Scotland

History: The history of St Andrews is inextricably linked with the history of golf itself (see page 1). Before the mid-19th century, the same hole was played twice in the round, until the increasing popularity of the course forced the authorities to put two holes on each green. To this day, St Andrews has seven such 'double greens' for 14 of the course's holes, some measuring more than an acre!

Pocket Fact

Unlike the other oldest clubs, the R&A have always played on the same course since their inception, even though they don't actually own the course.

Tournaments played there: 27 Open Championships.

Famous events:

- 1970: Doug Sanders misses a three-foot putt for the Open (see page 135).

- 1990: Nick Faldo wins his second Open Championship after taking no more than two putts on every green.

- 2000: The then highest-ever Open Championship attendance sees Tiger Woods win by eight strokes after steering clear of every single bunker throughout the 72 holes.

Did you know? Golf was banned at St Andrews in 1457, as King James II felt it was distracting the country's young men from archery practice.

Course topography: St Andrews is the quintessential links course, laid out over rumpled expanses of grass and gorse as if by nature itself. It is not only the double greens that are vast: many of the fairways at St Andrews are extremely wide. However, this does not guarantee an easy ride; approach shots to the green can vary markedly in terms of difficulty depending where on the fairway you are playing from. The bunkers are small, deep and often situated in the middle of the fairways, forcing a decision about which direction to hit the tee shot.

Signature hole: 17th, 455 yards, par 4. Named the 'Road Hole' after the stretch of tarmac that runs past the back of the green, this may be the most famous golf hole in the world. The 'Road Bunker', a devilishly deep pothole with a brick face, lies at the front of the green to swallow up short approach shots. Even if you manage to land on the green, putts are extremely difficult to read and an over-hit putt could end up back in the bunker!

How do I get to play there? The Old Course is open to the public, with a maximum permitted handicap of 24 for men and 36 for women. A ballot is drawn each day for play the following day; alternatively, guaranteed tee times can be purchased at a premium price through the Old Course Experience. Green fees range from £64 to £130, depending on the season. If you are planning a visit, be aware that the course is usually closed on Sundays to let it 'rest'.

Pocket Caddie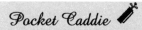

Befriend a student – they can join the club for a reduced fee!

Swilcan Bridge

One of golf's most famous photo opportunities, the Swilcan Bridge traverses the famous burn that runs across the shared fairway of the first and last holes at St Andrews. It was originally built by the Romans as part of the thoroughfare between the town and the harbour area in the Eden Estuary. Both Arnold Palmer and Jack Nicklaus waved goodbye to their British fans from the Swilcan Bridge, as both played their last Open Championships at St Andrews.

If you want to have your photo taken on the Swilcan Bridge, the best day to do it is Sunday, as you won't have to avoid flying balls!

Royal Birkdale

First played: 1897

Location: Southport, England

History: Royal Birkdale Golf Club was formed in 1889 on a 9-hole course, moving to its current 18-hole location at Birkdale Hills in 1897. Situated on England's north-west coast, the course benefited from a redesigning of all 18 greens in 1991.

Tournaments played there: Nine Open Championships, two Ryder Cups.

Famous events:

- 1969: The second Ryder Cup played at Royal Birkdale ends in a tie (see page 113).

- 1971: Lee Trevino wins the 100th Open after a final-day battle with the Taiwanese golfer, Lu Liang-Huan, known as 'Mr Lu'.

- 2008: Padraig Harrington successfully defends the Open Championship, overhauling Greg Norman who led going into the final round.

Did you know? Royal Birkdale has traditionally been one of the more enlightened golf clubs: women were allowed to use the links from the first year the course was open.

Course topography: Royal Birkdale is a classic links course, unevenly contoured with plenty of scrub and sand dunes. The fairways are laid out in flat-bottomed valleys between the towering dunes, which double as superb viewing galleries during tournaments. No two holes face in the same direction, presenting a particular challenge in the frequently windy conditions. Overlooking the 18th green is an art-deco clubhouse, built in the 1930s and intended to resemble an ocean liner cruising through the landscape.

Signature hole: 16th, 439 yards, par 4. This dog-leg hole demands an exceptional approach shot to get onto the green in two: the green sits on a plateau with very deep bunkers and hollows on both sides. Trees behind the green have been removed to make the approach shot harder to judge.

How do I get to play there? Visitors can play the course, but only on some days of the week. Green fees range from £120 to £195 per round, depending on the time of year.

Pocket Fact 🏌

In the 1961 Open Championship, Arnold Palmer's second shot on the 16th hole into fierce gales was so good that a plaque was mounted on the fairway to commemorate it.

Ballybunion (Old Course)

First played: 1893

Location: County Kerry, Ireland

History: The Ballybunion Golf Club originally closed in 1898 due to financial pressures, but rose again phoenix-like in 1906, and by 1927 the links had been extended to 18 holes. It was not until 1957, when it first hosted the Irish Professional Championship, that the course came to prominence.

Tournaments played there: Irish Open, Palmer Cup.

Did you know? The town of Ballybunion was named after the Bunion family, who owned the local castle dating from the 15th century.

Course topography: Set against the stark and beautiful backdrop of the Atlantic Ocean, Ballybunion is a testament to the power of nature. The rolling contours of the fairways and the largest sand dunes in Ireland demand accurate (and sometimes blind) approach shots that take into account the Atlantic wind.

Signature hole: 11th, 453 yards, par 4. Tom Watson once described this hole as: 'The best par 4 in the world'. The tee is set just above the beach on a flattened dune, with beautiful views of the estuary. The fairway is split into three by wild grasses, with ocean to the right and dunes to the left, so you won't benefit just from being able to hit it long.

How do I get to play there? Although Ballybunion is a private members' club, visitors are welcome to play. Booking in advance is essential – in previous years the course has been booked up for the summer season by the end of February. The maximum permitted handicap is 28 for men and 36 for women. Green fees range from €65 to €180 (approx. £55–£150) depending on the time of year.

Pocket Fact

Bill Clinton played golf here during his visit to Ireland in 1998.

Carnoustie (Championship Course)

First played: 1850

Location: Angus, Scotland.

History: The present course was first designed by Alan Robertson of St Andrews in 1850, extended by Old Tom Morris in 1867, and redesigned by James Braid in 1926. Finally, the last three holes were reinvented in 1937 to produce one of the toughest finishing stretches in golf.

Tournaments played there: Seven Open Championships, two Scottish Opens, Walker Cup.

Famous events:

- 1953: Ben Hogan wins the Open on his first visit to Scotland. The narrow gap between bunkers and out of bounds on the 6th hole is known as 'Hogan's Alley' after his perfectly directed shot.

- 1975: Tom Watson wins the last 18-hole play-off in Open history.

- 1999: Jean Van de Velde takes an unscheduled detour into the water (see page 136).

Did you know? Carnoustie boasts the first named commoner golfer: in a reference from 1527, one Sir Robert Maule is said to have 'exercisit the gowf [played golf]', but only 'when the wager was for drink'.

Course topography: Carnoustie has been nicknamed 'The Beast', in recognition of its famously ferocious nature when the wind is blowing. It is also strikingly beautiful, with gorse colouring the open fairways and rolling dunes framing the greens. With a daunting mixture of bunkers and burns, Carnoustie is renowned as one of the toughest of British courses.

Signature hole: 14th, 514 yards, par 5. The hole is guarded by the famous 'Spectacles' bunkers, lurking side by side 80 yards from the green. Their position demands a long tee shot in order for the second shot to be able to carry them – but the tee shot is imperilled by the out of bounds on the left and a wood to the right. Gary Player clinched victory in the 1968 Open by leaving his 3-wood approach three feet from the hole – still referred to by locals as 'The Shot'.

How do I get to play there? Carnoustie is a public links course, so anyone can play. The maximum permitted handicap is 28 for men and 36 for women. Green fees are £130.

Pocket Fact 🏌

The last three Open Championships at Carnoustie have all required play-offs to decide the winner.

Kingsbarns

First played: 1793

Location: Fife, Scotland

History: Golf was originally played on the links land of Kingsbarns from 1793, until the land was ploughed for farming in 1850. The course was first resurrected in 1922 as a 9-hole structure, but closed again after being mined by the allies during the Second World War. American architect, Kyle Phillips, recently rebuilt the course to almost universal acclaim.

Tournaments played there: The Alfred Dunhill Links Championship, a pro-am tournament.

Did you know? The course was commandeered by the Army during the Second World War in order to prevent an invasion from its coast.

Course topography: Kingsbarns enjoys omnipresent North-Sea views, made possible by the 'amphitheatre' structure of the course, which slopes towards the sea. Elevated tees give you a clear idea of the dangers ahead – there are burns, hollows, and pot bunkers – and the greens are fast and infuriatingly contoured. The clubhouse provides dramatic, panoramic views over both the ocean and the course.

Signature hole: 18th, par 4, 444 yards. A truly epic final hole. The uphill approach shot is everything, as the green is perched beyond a deep burn which flows down to the shoreline – so anything short is likely to end up on its way out to sea! That this drama is played out right in front of the clubhouse only enhances the psychological test.

How do I get to play there? The course is open for booking from April to October. Green fees range from £145 to £165 depending on the time of year.

Pocket Fact

Kingsbarns was the first new Scottish links course to be built for 70 years.

Royal Portrush (Dunluce Links)

First played: 1929

Location: County Antrim, Northern Ireland

History: Named after the ruined 13th-century castle that overlooks the course, Dunluce Links was created by Harry Colt (see page 79), who considered it his finest work. Within a year of opening, the Dunluce course hosted the Irish Open; and, after it became the first Irish course to host the Open Championship in 1951, the stage was set for the quiet, fishing village of Portrush to become an international golfing destination.

Tournaments played there: Open Championship.

Did you know? If you feel in need of liquid refreshment after a gruelling round, you are in luck: nearby Bushmills is the world's oldest-working whiskey distillery, having first been granted a licence in 1608.

Course topography: The course sits on a triangle of rugged links land on the North Antrim Causeway Coast, and constantly changes in both direction and elevation, with some of the most jaw-dropping scenery to be found in Ireland forming a constant backdrop. The course is renowned for its brutal rough: rumpled fairways twist through towering sand dunes; and testing greens are protected by grassy hummocks rather than bunkers, combined with the unpredictable winds roaring in off the North Atlantic.

Signature hole: 5th, 411 yards, par 4. The hole doglegs from the elevated tee through rough and sea grasses. Take care with your approach shot, as the White Rocks beach lurks behind the green.

How do I get to play there? Visitors are welcomed on both the Dunluce and Valley Links courses, as long as they hold a current handicap – maximum 18 for men and 24 for women. Green fees for Dunluce range from £60 to £140 depending on the time of year.

Pocket Fact ⚑
Fred Daly, the only Irishman ever to win the British Open, was a member at Royal Portrush.

Royal Dornoch (Championship Course)
First played: 1616
Location: Sutherland, Scotland

Pocket Fact

Tom Watson played Royal Dornoch after winning the Open at Muirfield in 1981, and went round two more times after having 'the most fun I've ever had on a golf course'. Watson is now an Honorary Member, along with HRH Prince Andrew, and fellow-golfer and course-designer Ben Crenshaw.

History: Written records date golfing at Dornoch as early as 1616 – making it the third-oldest golfing location in Scotland, behind St Andrews and Leith. By 1889, a full 18-hole course had been designed by local experts, among them Old Tom Morris. The course has undergone a series of changes over the years, having been closed for military use during the Second World War with an aerodrome being built on the ladies' course.

Did you know? A stone standing in one Dornoch garden commemorates Scotland's last witch-burning in 1722 (although some records put the date at 1727). The 'crime' of Janet Horne, the alleged witch, was to have borne a baby with a deformed hand.

Course topography: Royal Dornoch's hallmarks are the product of the incredible natural landscape in which it is set: magnificent contours and undulations, flowering gorse which sets the fairways ablaze with colour in summer, and raised greens which make approach play especially challenging. Nothing is hidden and there is plenty of room on both fairways and greens, albeit accompanied by thick rough and thoughtful bunkering, but positioning is all-important.

Pocket Caddie

As the front nine holes share greens with the back nine, take note of as many pin placements as possible – the greens are so large from front to back that this knowledge could make a big difference to approach shots later in the round.

Signature hole: 14th, 445 yards, par 4. The appropriately named 'Foxy' compensates for being the only hole without a bunker with a bewildering range of natural defences, from the 'double dog-leg' fairway – narrowed by wild dunes from the left and a series of rough-strewn hillocks on the right – to the narrow, plateau green with a steep fall-off on one side.

How do I get to play there? The course is open to the public, although some tee times are reserved for members. Green fees range from £40 to £95 depending on the time of year. There is a handicap limit of 24 for men and 35 for women.

Pocket Caddie

If you are planning to play there, remember to allow plenty of travel time – Dornoch's remote location in the northern Highlands is one of the reasons why the course has not hosted the British Open.

Wentworth (West Course)

First played: 1926

Location: Surrey, England

History: Of the three championship courses that now nestle in the Surrey heathland, the most famous is the West Course, designed shortly after the neighbouring East Course by Harry Colt. To the West Course fell the honour of hosting the major tournaments such as the Ryder Cup and the World Match Play Championship.

Tournaments played there: Ryder Cup, PGA Championship, World Match Play Championship.

Famous events:

- 1926: Last match played between Great Britain and the US before being officially recognised as the Ryder Cup.

- 1953: The 10th Ryder Cup is played at Wentworth. The US wins a closely-fought match $6\frac{1}{2}$–$5\frac{1}{2}$.

Did you know? Below the course hides a secret wartime HQ – Wentworth was allowed to grow wild during the Second World War to deter enemy aircraft from landing on the fairways.

Course topography: Colt's design for the West Course is one of variety: holes differ in elevation, the fairways wind this way and that through the oak and pine, and the golfer is confronted with both short and long holes. The course has recently been redesigned by club professional, Ernie Els, to bring it into the modern era.

Signature hole: 17th, 566 yards, par 5. The trees clustered on either side make the hole seem dauntingly narrow from the tee. Many golfers are so anxious to avoid the out of bounds on the left of the fairway that they hit to the right, where the fairway slopes sharply down towards thick rough and trees.

How do I get to play there? The course is open to the public from Monday to Friday. A current handicap certificate is required.

Pocket Fact

Wentworth can claim to be the birthplace of golf's most famous competition: the Ryder Cup.

Loch Lomond

First played: 1993

Location: Dunbartonshire, Scotland

History: Loch Lomond Golf Club is built on land still owned by the ancestral lairds, the Clan Colquhoun, whose estate dates back to the 12th century. The clubhouse is a Georgian manor house, built in 1773.

Tournaments played there: Scottish Open since 1996.

Did you know? Architect, Tom Weiskopf, the 1973 Open champion, was almost literally consumed by his creation: he went out to survey the land prior to construction one morning, only to sink up to his chin in quicksand. Fortunately he survived to complete the course Nick Faldo has called 'the finest in Europe'.

Course topography: Nestled between the famous loch and the mountains, the course is strikingly beautiful, particularly the front nine with their spectacular views of the loch. The back nine represent a more challenging series of holes that take you inland through the swampy area where Weiskopf got stuck. As befits an exclusive club, the course is immaculately maintained, with verdant fairways and flawless greens, and the tree-lined setting keeps each hole in a world of its own.

Signature hole: 6th hole, 625 yards, par 5. The longest hole in Scottish golf plays alongside the 'bonnie banks' of the loch. A cannily positioned fairway bunker anticipates your second shot and the green is raised against a backdrop of water.

How do I get to play there? With difficulty: you need to be invited by an existing member or by the club itself, and only 15,000 rounds are played each year – a third of the average for courses of similar stature.

Pocket Fact

The Loch Lomond course contains three Sites of Special Scientific Interest (so designated to protect rare plants and unusual woodland).

Sunningdale (Old Course)

First played: 1901

Location: Berkshire, England

History: Double Open winner Willie Park Jr designed the Old Course: the most famous of Sunningdale's two courses.

Tournaments played there: Walker Cup (1987), International Final Qualifying for the British Open.

Did you know? During the First World War troops based nearby were allowed access to the clubhouse.

Course topography: The course was designed on barren heathland, so the original soil had to be entirely imported from elsewhere. The fairways are lined with heather and trees, and 103 bunkers are scattered throughout the course. The greens are deceptively contoured and in immaculate condition.

Signature hole: 5th, 407 yards, par 4. The elevated tee affords a wonderful view of the heather and forests bordering the fairway. Bunkers are stationed both on the fairway and around the green, and a pond stands in the way of the second shot to the green.

How do I get to play there? Sunningdale is open to visitors from Monday to Thursday. Green fees are £115–£190 depending on the time of year.

EUROPE

Valderrama

Awesome.

Fred Couples, upon seeing Valderrama for the first time

First played: 1974 (under the name Sotogrande)

Location: Cadiz, Spain

History: Frustrated by overcrowding at the old Sotogrande course, a group of residents decided to take matters into their own hands. The 'New' course was designed by renowned golf architect, Robert Trent Jones Sr, in 1974, and renamed Valderrama after the ancient estate on which the land is situated by new owner, Jaime Ortiz-Patiño.

Tournaments played there: 1997 Ryder Cup, Volvo Masters.

Famous events: 1997: Europe recapture the Ryder Cup.

Did you know? Valderrama is the only course outside Britain and the US to host the Ryder Cup.

Course topography: Valderrama could be viewed as the European equivalent of Augusta, with ubiquitous cork-oak trees, lush fairways, and stunning views of the surrounding countryside and distant Mediterranean. Valderrama is also relatively short, but this doesn't mean it's an easy course to play: picturesque hazards abound, making positioning critical to every shot.

Signature hole: 4th, 516 yards, par 5. Called 'La Cascada' after the waterfall on the lake set beside the two-tiered green. The opportunity is there to go for the green in two, but with the lake across the back and right, the penalty can be severe. Strategically positioned bunkers add to the challenge.

How do I get to play there? Valderrama is a private members' club, but a limited number of starting times are offered for visitors on most days of the year, with a maximum handicap of 24 for men and 32 for women. Green fees are €300–€320 (approx. £280–£300).

Pocket Caddie 🏌

The course is a cash-free zone: you need to fund a special Smart Card to make a purchase, with the balance being refunded on departure.

Les Bordes

First played: 1986

Location: Loire Valley, France

History: Les Bordes was the joint venture of Baron Bich, who owns the surrounding estate, and Yoshiaki Sakurai, a Japanese businessman. The course was designed by American golf architect, Robert von Hagge, and opened in 1987.

Did you know? Les Bordes' co-founder, Baron Marcel Bich, is also the founder of the BIC manufacturing empire.

Course topography: Set in the serene woodlands of the Loire Valley, the course is subtly crafted to blend in with its natural surroundings, with fast, contoured greens guarded by vast bunkers – and also by expanses of water on 12 of the 18 holes – at the end of undulating tree-lined fairways. So while playing Les Bordes is both a tranquil and exhilarating experience, it is also a challenging one: the course record is only one stroke below par!

Signature hole: 16th, 215 yards, par 3. Although the only short hole without water, the 16th is one of the course's toughest. Your tee shot must contend with a huge bunker set front-right of the green – however, an even worse fate is to be too long, as the back of the green slopes away dramatically.

How do I get to play there? Les Bordes is a private club, so you may only play as guests of an existing member. The new owners have commissioned von Hagge to build two further courses as part of a resort complex, which will be open to non-members.

Pocket Fact

Les Bordes has the largest putting green in Europe, with 36 separate holes. French sculptor, Augustine Rodin, created the wild boar that watches over the practising players.

PGA Catalunya (Stadium Course)

First played: 1999

Location: Girona, Spain

History: The Stadium Course (formerly known as the Green Course) was designed and built at the behest of the European Tour to stand comparison to the Sawgrass Course on the US PGA Tour.

Tournaments played there: Spanish Open.

Did you know? The Stadium Course is the only course to have hosted two European Tour events within 10 months of opening.

Course topography: The course is set in a large, pine forest on rolling hills, at the foot of the Pyrenees. Unsurprisingly, the result is visually spectacular: the course is notable for its elevated tees and downhill holes, with both stunning views and hazards in panoramic sight. The nature of the course is apparent from the

1st tee: pine trees, scrub and purple heather line the fairways. The greens are immaculate, contoured, and bunkered with white powdery sand, while lakes feature on seven of the holes.

Signature hole: 2nd, 354 yards, par 4. Although short, this hole punches above its weight: the fairway gets narrower the further you hit off the tee, tapering into a 'moat' of rough around the raised green.

How do I get to play there? Green fees for casual players are €80–€120 (approx. £70–£110) depending on the time of year. Advance booking is recommended and proof of handicap is required (maximum 28 for men and 36 for women). A second course, known as the Tour Course, offers a similarly beautiful but less demanding challenge for the higher-handicap golfer.

Morfontaine

First played: 1913 (Championship Course first played 1927)

Location: Morfontaine, France

History: The first golf course at Morfontaine was the nine-hole Valliere course, built at the behest of the landowner, the Duke of Guiche, who had previously used the land for polo. Tom Simpson was subsequently commissioned to design the 18-hole championship course, which has recently been updated by Kyle Phillips.

Did you know? Morfontaine was commandeered by the Third Reich during the occupation of France in 1940: many greens and fairways were damaged by tanks, shells and cannon.

Course topography: Morfontaine is situated in the middle of birch and pine forests, and every hole is heavily wooded. Despite its inland location the soil is extremely sandy – which means the course plays fast and hard like a links course, complete with rolling, heathland fairways. Most of the bunkers are deep and clustered around the greens, which vary formidably in the degree of contouring.

Signature hole: 7th, 428 yards, par 4. A blind, uphill tee shot over a belt of heather and rocks leads you into a sharp left dog-leg. If you can cut the corner over the trees, you are rewarded with a short, downhill approach to the undulating green – but as the fairway slopes dramatically left to right this can be difficult to secure.

How do I get to play there? Morfontaine is famously private, and only members' guests may play the course. It is also hard to find, as it is located down a series of side roads in a forest area.

Pocket Fact 🚩

Morfontaine has played host to royalty since the Second World War: the King of Spain, the King of Belgium and the Duke of Windsor all played rounds here.

Halmstad (North Course)

First played: 1938

Location: Halmstad, Sweden

History: The two Halmstad courses are the combined creation of renowned designers, Rafael Sundblom, Nils Sköld and Frank Pennink. Sundblom designed the original course in 1935, and Sköld added nine holes in 1963, which were combined with the last nine holes of the old course to complete the magnificent 18-hole layout of the North Course. Pennink added nine holes in 1975, which were combined with the first nine holes of the old course to produce the less heralded South Course.

Tournaments played there: PGA Open Championship, Solheim Cup.

Did you know? The nearby Tylösand Hotel is co-owned by Swedish pop star, Per Gessle, who was born in Halmstad: Roxette memorabilia line the walls of the bar.

Course topography: Situated in pine forests bordering the Swedish coastline, the North Course winds down long, wooded fairways, each seemingly in complete isolation: in fact, there are so many trees that rough is rendered unnecessary. The many and varied obstacles include sloping fairways, ravines, streams and fast, plateau greens, all kept in pristine condition throughout the year despite the long winters.

Signature hole: 16th, 179 yards, par 3. Voted Sweden's best golf hole in 2004, 'The Brook' is named after the creek that winds all the way from tee to green, cutting across the fairway from left to right.

How do I get to play there? Halmstad is open for anyone to play – booking in advance is recommended. Green fees are 600SEK (approx. £55).

USA

Pine Valley

First played: 1919

Location: New Jersey, USA

History: Pine Valley was made possible by George Crump, a Philadelphian hotel owner, dissatisfied with the quality of courses in his area. He started work on the previously desolate scrubland in 1913, seeking Harry Colt's advice, and had completed most of the holes by his death in 1918. Hugh Wilson completed the remaining holes, and the course was opened the following year to great anticipation and acclaim.

Tournaments played there: Two Walker Cups.

Did you know? Crump lived alone on the course for five years during construction.

Course topography: The course possesses an extraordinary diversity of challenges, from the bunker-less first green with its three-sided slope, to the final hole's brilliant synthesis of the course's finest characteristics, laid out before you from the elevated tee. Vast expanses of bunker and scrub, thickly clustered trees, sloping fairways and superbly shaped greens combine to test not only the golfer's skill but also their mind. Most of the drives and approach shots are required to carry over sand, water, or scrub.

Signature hole: 7th, 580 yards, par 5. The flattest hole on the course boasts its most infamous hazard: Hell's Half Acre, a sandy wasteland that bisects the fairway for nearly 100 yards from the halfway point. The size of the dune piles pressure onto your second shot, but also forces you to lay it up short if your tee shot lands in the rough. Past Hell's Half Acre, the green is formidably contoured.

How do I get to play there? You need to be invited by a member to play at Pine Valley. Non-members are allowed access to walk the course during the annual Crump Cup, the club championship, every October.

Pocket Fact

The club's members used to offer a bet to first-time players that they wouldn't shoot less than 80 — until a young Arnold Palmer cleaned them out in 1954 by hitting 68.

Cypress Point

It is the only course I know where one literally gasps with astonishment at its beauty.
Dr Alister MacKenzie, Cypress Point architect

First played: 1928

Location: California, USA

History: Cypress Point Golf Club was formed in 1926, but it was not until the original designer, Seth Raynor, died later that year that Alister MacKenzie was approached. MacKenzie, acutely aware of the land's potential, didn't require much persuading.

Tournaments played there: Walker Cup (1981).

Did you know? A scene from the Hitchcock film, *Vertigo,* was filmed just south of the clubhouse on 17-Mile Drive.

Course topography: Set on the tip of the Monterey Peninsula and overlooking the Pacific Ocean, Cypress Point is more than the equal of its famous neighbour, Pebble Beach. The 'scene stealing' holes are those set on the clifftops alongside the ocean, but the rest of the course is of a similarly high standard: a journey through wooded, inland hillside and open dunes nearer the sea. The distinctive cypress trees, with their twisted trunks and 'sculpted' foliage, define the course as much as the famous sea views, while man-made bunkers blend seamlessly with the natural dunes.

Signature hole: 16th, 231 yards, par 3. From the tee you are presented with one of the most staggering and daunting views in golf: your drive to the green, jutting out into Monterey Bay on a rocky peninsula, must carry 200 yards over the Pacific Ocean itself. Despite the extreme difficulty of this hole, it was once 'aced' by Bing Crosby in 1947!

How do I get to play there? You need to be invited by a member – and as there were only 250 of these at the last count, this may take some doing!

Pocket Fact
The club is so exclusive that, according to local legend, John F Kennedy was once refused entry to the restaurant.

Augusta National

To think this ground has been lying here all these years, waiting for someone to come along and lay a golf course on it.
Bobby Jones

First played: 1933

Location: Georgia, USA

History: Augusta represented the collaboration between golf's leading architect, Alister MacKenzie, and its best player of the age, the recently retired Bobby Jones. The course was designed with a view to hosting the US Open, but this idea was ultimately discarded in favour of inaugurating a new invitation-only tournament. MacKenzie died only two months before the first US Masters in 1934, when Jones made his competitive return; Augusta has been home to the competition ever since.

Tournaments played there: US Masters (annually).

Famous events:

- 1958: Arnold Palmer wins his first Masters by a single shot in controversial circumstances, after a ruling allowed him to count the score of a second ball because his first had been 'embedded'.

- 1986: Jack Nicklaus astonishes the golf world by winning his final major at the age of 46 (see page 134).

- 1988: Sandy Lyle becomes the first British Masters champion (see page 134).

- 1997: Tiger Woods becomes the youngest-ever Masters winner in his first major, finishing 12 shots clear of the nearest competitor.

Did you know? Augusta National was designed on the site of a former indigo plantation; each hole is named after the diverse flora found around the course.

Course topography: Augusta was originally modelled on the Old Course at St Andrews, with fewer bunkers and wider fairways than were common at the time. However, due to frequent changes in the ensuing decades, today's course corresponds more closely to American tastes, with the fairways cleanly cropped and populated by pines, creeks and sculpted bunkers of white sand. The greens are dangerously fast and there are undulations throughout. Recent revisions have lengthened the course to protect against modern advancements.

Signature hole: 12th, 155 yards, par 3. This deceptively tranquil spot is in the middle of Augusta's famous trio of holes, known as Amen Corner. The narrow green, perched on the far side of Rae's Creek (a wide stream which runs across the fairway) with a steep, bunkered hill of trees and azaleas behind, is made for the theatre of a major tournament.

How do I get to play there? Augusta National is one of the most exclusive golf clubs in the world, with around 300 members who, along with the current holder of the Masters title, are allowed to wear the coveted Green Jacket. You can play only if invited by a member.

Pocket Fact

The Eisenhower Pine on the 17th hole is so named after the then US President, a club member, proposed in 1956 that it be cut down because he had hit it so many times . . . at which point the meeting was tactfully adjourned.

Pebble Beach Golf Links

> *If I only had one more round to play, I would choose to play at Pebble Beach.*
> Jack Nicklaus

First played: 1919

Location: California, USA

History: Pebble Beach Golf Links came into being as a way of divesting the land holdings of the Pacific Improvement Company. The designers, amateur golfers, Jack Neville and Douglas Grant, were tasked with combining the amazing scenery with a challenging layout. Henry Chandler Egan remodelled the course in 1928, and Jack Nicklaus has also made minor modifications.

Tournaments played there: Five US Open Championships (including 2010), PGA Championship (1977).

Famous events:

- 1972: Jack Nicklaus hits one of the most famous golf shots ever on the penultimate hole of the US Open, a 1-iron in high winds that hits the flag and stops five inches from the hole.

- 1982: Tom Watson, currently tied with Nicklaus, chips in from the rough on the very same hole for a birdie that propels him to US Open victory.

- 2000: Tiger Woods wins the 100th US Open by 15 strokes with the joint lowest-ever 72-hole score in the tournament.

Did you know? The nearby Hotel Del Monte is responsible for the original usage of the famous Del Monte canned-fruit brand.

Course topography: The course is routed along the rugged cliffs above Carmel Bay, which provides a spectacular backdrop to the most famous holes. But Pebble Beach is not only celebrated for its scenery: the course is notoriously challenging, with strong headwinds and the thundering of the Pacific combined with small, fast and sloping greens. Away from the cliffs, the holes are lined with pine and cypress trees.

Signature hole: 18th, 543 yards, par 5. One of the most famous finishing holes in golf, with the Pacific Ocean thundering into the crescent of rocks all the way down the left side. The ideal line is as close to the ocean as possible, with a pair of trees bisecting the fairway and another blocking the right-hand side of the green. Beware of the long bunker that runs alongside the ocean to the green for over 100 yards.

How do I get to play there? The good news is that anyone is able to play Pebble Beach – the bad news is that green fees are $495 (approx. £342) per round. It's also advisable to book in plenty of time – up to two or three months in advance in summer.

Pocket Fact 🏌

Since 1947, Pebble Beach has hosted the annual 'Crosby Clambake'.

Shinnecock Hills

First played: 1891

Location: New York, USA

History: In 1890, a group of Long-Island locals on holiday in Biarritz happened upon Scottish professional, Willie Dunn, who was constructing a golf course. Dunn was subsequently hired to design a course in the rolling dunes of Shinnecock, enlisting 150 Native Americans from the nearby Shinnecock Reservation to help him. Toomey and Flynn redesigned the course extensively in 1928.

Tournaments played there: Four US Opens, Walker Cup (1977).

Did you know? Shinnecock Hills boasted the first golf clubhouse in the US.

Course topography: The course is constructed in a links style, with sweeping fairways, thick rough lining the fairways and numerous fairway bunkers. The challenges are subtle and rely on an understanding of the conditions as well as the terrain. For example, the longer par-4 holes are downwind, enabling 'bump and run' shots onto the undulating greens, while the shorter ones have tighter targets but play into the wind, allowing more-controlled approach shots.

Signature hole: 7th, 189 yards, par 3. A classic 'Redan' hole (a par 3 with a diagonally sloping green). Your tee shot into the prevailing wind hits a green that slopes from front-right to back-left – anything landing on the left side rolls down to a flat area behind the hole.

How do I get to play there? You need to be invited by a member.

Pocket Fact

In 1896, Shinnecock Hills hosted the first US Open to allow African American and Native American golfers to compete alongside Caucasians golfers.

The most unusual places to play golf

- ***Play it cool (Greenland)**. The World Ice Golf Championship takes place every March in the small town of Uummannaq, 370 miles from the Arctic Circle. The course plays differently from one year to the next, as the ice floes* upon which it is designed are continually changing. The golf balls are red and the green is white. Dress appropriately if you're going, as temperatures can fall to −50°C!

- **Cross-country golf (Sweden/Finland)**. The Green Zone golf club, straddling the border between Sweden and Finland, is currently the world's only transnational golf course.

- **Golf's largest sand trap (Australia)**. The mining town of Coober Pedy, in South Australia, is famous for two things: the locals live underground to avoid the unrelenting heat, and its golf course consists entirely of sand — the only patch of grass being the one you carry with you to tee off from. The majority of golf takes place during the night, using glowing golf balls.

- **Hit the heights (South Africa)**. The 'Extreme 19th Hole' of the Legend Golf Resort in South Africa has a tee-box that sits over 1,400 feet above the green. The tee is reached by helicopter and the ball takes an average of nearly 30 seconds to drop onto the green below. If you hole this in one, it's worth $1m!

- **Golf around the clock (Alaska)**. Can't get enough golf? The North Star Golf Club in Fairbanks, Alaska, is open 20 hours a day in the summer months — it is America's northernmost golf club so the sun shines around the clock in the summer months.

- **Lose yourself (China)**. Mission Hills in Shenzhen, China — the world's largest golf complex with 12 championship courses across 20 square kilometres, each course designed by top PGA professionals.

- **Bunkers . . . of the military variety (in the demilitarised zone separating North and South Korea)**. 'The world's most dangerous golf course' consists of a single par-3 hole with an AstroTurf green, where out of bounds is delineated by barbed wire. A sign on the tee reads: 'Danger! Do not retrieve balls from the rough. Live mine fields.'

- *The world's most unpredictable green (USA).* The world's only floating green is found on the 14th hole of the Coeur-d'Alene-Resort course in Idaho. A dedicated Putter-Boat shuttle ferries the players to and from the shore.

Pocket Fact ⚑

Coober Pedy is the only course whose members have reciprocal playing rights with St Andrews. The catch is that it is with the Balgove course, a pedestrian 9-hole track, rather than the Old Course itself.

REST OF THE WORLD

Royal Melbourne (West Course)

First played: 1931

Location: Victoria, Australia

History: Although formed by 100 subscribers in 1891, the Royal Melbourne club only moved to its current home at Black Rock in 1930. The West Course, designed by Dr Alister MacKenzie, opened the following year, and the East Course the year after that. A 'composite' 18-hole course, used for championship golf, draws 12 of the holes from the West.

Tournaments played there: Three World Cups (previously Canada Cup), several Australian Opens, Presidents' Cup.

Course topography: The course is accessible to all standards of golfer, with wider fairways and larger greens than many modern courses, and no water hazards. However, shot placement is all-important to be able to attack the devilishly undulating greens while avoiding the brilliantly positioned bunkers. The West Course is designed to encourage a risk strategy – and not always to reward length.

Signature hole: 5th, 176 yards, par 3. The view from the tee is daunting: beyond a sand-covered valley, an intimidating cluster of bunkers eats into the green, at the front of which is a steep bank to punish short tee shots. Even an accurate tee shot does not ensure safety: the lightning-fast green visibly tilts from back to front.

How do I get to play there? Visitors from overseas or interstate can play the course during the week, by presenting a letter of introduction from their club secretary. Bookings should be made well in advance. Maximum handicap is 27 for men and 45 for women.

Pocket Fact

Dr MacKenzie never saw the finished version of his design.

Kingston Heath

First played: 1925

Location: Victoria, Australia

History: Located in Melbourne's south-eastern suburbs, Kingston Heath was designed by former Australian Open champion, Dan Soutar, and featured bunkering by Dr Alister MacKenzie. When it opened for play in 1925, Kingston Heath was the longest course in Australia.

Tournaments played there: Seven Australian Opens, seven Australian Match Play Championships, Women's Australian Open.

Famous events:

- 1983: Peter Fowler causes one of the great Australian golf upsets, to win the Australian Open ahead of David Graham and Ian Baker-Finch.

- 2000: In his first season as a professional, Melbourne local, Aaron Baddeley defends the Open title he won as an amateur the previous year.

Did you know? The course narrowly escaped obliteration in 1944: a large bushfire spread throughout the undergrowth and rough, and the clubhouse was spared only by a sudden wind change.

Course topography: While its length is no longer so daunting in the modern era, Kingston Heath's design has stood the test of time: its natural bunkering, dips and hollows can be deceptive. The course itself is highly sculpted, thick rough and sandy grasses severely punish errant drives.

Signature hole: 15th, 155 yards, par 3. Changed from a short par 4 on MacKenzie's advice, the hole plays uphill where deep bunkers in front and to the right of the green seem to dwarf the target. Aiming anywhere other than the centre of the green is a high-risk strategy – and once you are on it, the undulating green presents a final test.

How do I get to play there? Kingston Heath is a private course, and guests must be accompanied by a member. Visitors from overseas or interstate are allowed to play on certain week-days, with a letter of introduction from their home club. Green fees are $330 (approx. £140–£150).

Pocket Fact 𝕀

For bunkering plans that he finished in days, MacKenzie received 10 times the fee paid to the course's designer.

Cape Kidnappers

First played: 2004

Location: Hawkes Bay, New Zealand

History: Cape Kidnappers was brought into being through the investment of American mogul, Julian Robertson, who purchased the land and handed it over to acclaimed designer, Tom Doak.

Did you know? The 5,000 acres on which Cape Kidnappers is built was previously a sheep station.

Course topography: Cape Kidnappers is set on seven natural 'fingers' of land that jut out to the edge of the cliffs, forming a breathtaking landscape of ridges and ravines. Unlike cliff-top courses such as Cypress Point, which plays along the shoreline, the holes at Cape Kidnappers are routed to and from the edge, with Hawkes Bay lying 140 metres below. The sea winds and firm ground make for an epic experience.

Signature hole: 6th, 225 yards, par 3. A stunning tee shot crosses one of the plunging ravines to the green beyond. A miss to the left puts you at the mercy of four bunkers – and that's if you're lucky, as they skirt the cliffs themselves. The 'safe' option to the right brings another two bunkers into play, and the green slopes from right to left.

How do I get to play there? The course is open to the public: green fees are NZ$300–NZ$400 (approx. £140–£190) depending on the time of year.

Pocket Fact 🏌

Cape Kidnappers was so named by Captain James Cook, after the Maori inhabitants tried to abduct a member of his crew there in 1769.

Casa de Campo (Teeth of the Dog Course)

I created 11 holes and God created seven!
Pete Dye, course architect

First played: 1971

Location: La Romana, Dominican Republic

History: Casa de Campo ('country house' in Spanish) is a tropical, seaside resort, originally developed on land owned by Gulf+Western so the company's founder could entertain his friends. The Casa has since been opened to paying guests who can enjoy no fewer than three separate courses, but Teeth of the Dog, winding alternately past palm trees and spectacular, ocean views, is the premier attraction.

Did you know? Teeth of the Dog was originally carved out of the jungle by 300 local labourers using machetes.

Course topography: Named after the jagged rocks lurking beside the seven ocean-front holes, Teeth of the Dog is a uniquely intimidating experience. Errant balls bounce crazily off ocean rocks, to be collected and sold back to golfers by local children; waste areas creep into the wind-blown fairways; and the fast, elevated greens are bordered by pot bunkers and the roaring Atlantic.

Pocket Caddie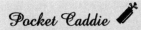

Play Teeth of the Dog in the afternoon – the 17th hole offers spectacular-sunset views over the ocean.

Signature hole: 16th hole, 204 yards, par 3. The dog bares its teeth on this hole – a cove shaped like snapping jaws is between you and the flag, forcing your tee shot to carry over the frothing ocean. A series of stepped bunkers in front of the green catches anything short that avoids the water: more sand awaits those who overshoot.

How do I get to play there? The course is open to the public, and advance bookings are recommended. Green fees are $200 (approx. £135).

Pocket Fact

The course gained popularity after it served as a backdrop for the 1971 Sports Illustrated Swimsuit Issue.

Leopard Creek
First played: 1996

Location: Mpumalanga, South Africa

History: South African golfer, Gary Player, created Leopard Creek with banker, Johann Rupert, in 1995, incorporating the

African bushveld (the sub-tropical scrubland of southern Africa) into a course that tests the most accomplished golfer.

Did you know? Think twice before retrieving your ball from the water – Leopard Creek's waterways are populated by crocodiles and hippos.

Course topography: With views from the clubhouse overlooking the Kruger National Park, Leopard Creek is a fusion of golf and safari. The temperate climate of the area ensures an enjoyable all-year-round experience whenever you are planning to go.

Signature hole: 13th, 550 yards, par 5. Simultaneously challenging and strikingly beautiful, this hole is a microcosm of the course. A stream cuts across the fairway and runs down the left side all the way to the heavily bunkered plateau green, which itself offers spectacular views of the wildlife of Kruger Park across Crocodile River.

How do I get to play there? Non-members can play midweek – green fees are from ZAR 1,300 (approx. £120).

Pocket Fact 🏌

The world's longest golf course, Nullarbor Links, stretches across two states in Australia, and has been measured at 848 miles, with holes up to 50 miles apart! The course is intended to stimulate tourism in the Eyre-Highway region, one of the most barren regions of south-west Australia.

Famous designers

Most of the world's top golf courses are attributable to a small group of elite, legendary golf architects. Here are the key players in the history of golf-course design:

- *Old Tom Morris*. The father of golf-course design, involved in the creation of most of the greatest Scottish links courses.
- *Dr Alister MacKenzie*. The foremost architect during the 'Golden Age' of golf design, a genius at 'risk and reward' holes and natural bunkering. His masterpieces include Augusta National, Cypress Point, and the finest Australian golf courses.
- *Tom Simpson*. Flamboyant designer of courses in continental Europe in the early 20th century. Memorably quipped: 'A golf hole should either be more difficult than it looks or look more difficult than it is. It must never be what it looks.'
- *Harry Colt*. Had a hand in designing many classic courses in the early 20th century, from Muirfield to Pine Valley.
- *Jack Nicklaus*. Has designed over 300 golf courses, including Gleneagles, the course chosen for the 2014 Ryder Cup.
- *Tom Doak*. 'Minimalist' golf-course architect of the new school: advocates naturally formed courses such as Pacific Dunes and Cape Kidnapper.

TOP GOLF HOLIDAY DESTINATIONS

Golf is just about the best excuse for travel yet discovered.
Henry Longhurst

While it is every golfer's ambition to spend their holidays playing the world's best courses, the rest of the family may not always be so keen! Luckily, there are plenty of holiday destinations that combine great golf with other facilities and pursuits, ensuring that there is something for everyone. Here are some of the world's finest.

Kiawah Island Golf Resort

Location: South Carolina, USA

History: First developed in 1974, Kiawah Island has a plethora of excellent courses, all but one of which are equipped with junior tee markers during the summer. The exception is The Ocean Course – with good reason: it is one of the toughest resort golf courses in the country.

Did you know? The Ocean Course hosted the 1991 Ryder Cup, also known as the 'War on the Shore'.

How can the kids join in?

- Two-day junior golf camps are run for players aged 12 to 17.

- A special Family-Tee programme takes place on four of the resort's golf courses during the summer, from 5.00pm–6.30pm. Children under–17 can play for free with an adult.

Why will the rest of the family like it?

- Kiawah Island's idyllic location – 10-mile beachfront backed by inland marshes and forests – makes for a bewildering variety of outdoor activities, including sailing trips and bike or jeep hire. Other activities include oyster roasts and beach-bonfire parties.

- Children aged three to 11 can join 'Kamp Kiawah' for nature hikes, sandcastling, crafts and outdoor activities; while teens can meet at movie nights, a variety of other sports, and dances.

Gleneagles

Location: Perthshire, Scotland

History: The Gleneagles Hotel, opened in 1924 by the Caledonian Railway Company as a 'Riviera in the Highlands', became a fixed part of high society's summer calendar by the 1950s. The original courses, King's and Queen's, were designed by five-times Open champion, James Braid; the PGA Centenary Course, the venue for the 2014 Ryder Cup, was added in 1993.

Pocket Fact ⛳

In 1981, Gleneagles was the venue for the longest, successful, competitive golf putt ever televised: a 33-yard monster by Terry Wogan in a pro-celebrity TV programme on the BBC.

How can the kids join in?

- As well as the three championship courses, including the Ryder Cup course for 2014, there is a 9-hole par-3 track called the 'Wee Course', and a pitch-and-putt course with junior golf clubs available.

Why will the rest of the family like it?

- A wide variety of pursuits are available for kids, or 'Gleneaglets' as they are known in this resort, from junior off-roading in miniature Land-Rovers to 'Own a Pony' days.

Pocket Caddie 🏌️

Think carefully about which of the five tee-boxes you want to play from at Gleneagles – the PGA Centenary Course is the longest inland course in Scotland.

Four Seasons Nevis Resort

Location: Nevis, West Indies

History: The Nevis Course, designed by Robert Trent Jones Jr, was opened in 1991 and quickly became known as one of the finest courses in the Caribbean.

How can the kids join in?

- The resort is child-focused – kids are even given their own registration pack on arrival.

Why will the rest of the family like it?

- The Ocean and Garden Pools are located right in front of the 4 mile beach.

- The Kids for All Seasons centre allows the kids to explore pirate ships and tree houses. There is also a wide selection of supervised activity, from night-time turtle watching to banana boating!

Celtic Manor

Location: Wales

History: The original Manor House dates from the 19th century and was first opened as a hotel in 1982. The more modern Resort Hotel was added in 1999 to cater for the venue's increasing popularity. The golf course is set at the bottom of a valley, creating a spectacular natural backdrop for every hole.

Did you know? Celtic Manor was chosen to host the 2010 Ryder Cup.

Why will the rest of the family like it?

- There is a luxury health club and spa, a gym, dance studio, infinity pool and children's club.

- The Ryder Cup is expected to cement the Celtic Manor Resort as one of Europe's most desirable resorts.

Arabella Golf Course, Kleinmond

Location: Arabella, South Africa

History: Arabella's spacious fairways make it suitable for all standards of golfer. The course combines different elements of natural beauty – with mountain backdrops, lagoons and forests.

Did you know? Arabella borders the largest-natural lagoon in South Africa.

Why will the rest of the family like it?

- As well as spectacular mountain ranges, beaches and sweeping valleys, the Western-Cape region boasts top-quality wineries and cuisine.

Pocket Fact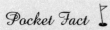

Graeme McDowell became Europe's first US Open Champion for 40 years after he won at Pebble Beach in June 2010. This was McDowell's first major title.

5

AT THE FORE:
FAMOUS GOLFERS

The rich history of professional golf is built on the characters who have led the field, from the early legends like Tom Morris, Bobby Jones and Sam Snead, through the post-war triumvirate of Palmer, Nicklaus and Player, to the modern greats such as Ballesteros, Norman and Woods. Here is an introduction to the players every golf fan should know.

◉ EARLY LEGENDS ◉

Old Tom Morris (1821–1908)

Nationality: Scottish

Big wins: Four Open Championships (1861, 1862, 1864, 1867)

What else was he famous for?

- Morris is known as the father of modern greenkeeping, and pioneered many ideas of turf and course management that are still in use today. Some of his course designs are still at the pinnacle of their rankings (see Chapter 4).

- Old Tom outlived all five of his children.

Did you know?

- Morris first played golf by knocking 'balls' made of wine-bottle corks pierced with nails around the streets of St Andrews.

- Morris formed a partnership, known as 'The Invincibles', with Allan Robertson who ran the St Andrews Links course – the two were the first and second to break 80 on the Old Course.

It was said that the pairing never lost a match played on even terms.

- Morris struck the first shot in the inaugural Open Championship of 1860.

- Morris is still the oldest winner of the Open Championship – his last victory coming at the age of 46.

- Devoted to St Andrews till the last, Morris met his death after falling down a flight of stairs at the clubhouse of the New Golf Club.

Young Tom Morris (1851–1875)

Nationality: Scottish

Big wins: Four Open Championships (1868, 1869, 1870, 1872)

Did you know?

- Young and Old Tom are the only father – son pairing to finish winner and runner-up in an Open Championship.

- Young Tom is responsible for the introduction of the famous Claret Jug, presented to the winner of the Open each year. His third victory in consecutive years entitled him to keep the original prize, the Championship Belt, forcing the authorities to commission a new trophy. The Claret Jug was first offered in 1872, and Young Tom was the first to win it with his fourth straight title!

- On his way to winning the 1869 Open, Young Tom scored the first-recorded tournament hole in one.

Walter Hagen (1892–1969)

Nationality: American

Nickname: Sir Walter

Big wins:

- Four Open Championships (1922, 1924, 1928, 1929)
- Two US Opens (1914, 1919)
- Five US PGAs (1921, 1924, 1925, 1926, 1927)

What else was he famous for?

- As the first full-time professional, touring the country to play exhibition matches, Hagen raised the status of professional players – who were looked upon at the time as a lower class of golfer.

- Hagen was one of the first players to endorse golf equipment.

Did you know? With his plus fours and two-tone shoes, Hagen was the first athlete to make the list of Best Dressed Americans.

Robert Tyre 'Bobby' Jones (1902–1971)

Nationality: American

Nickname: Bobby

Big wins:

- Four US Opens (1923, 1926, 1929, 1930)
- Three Open Championships (1926, 1927, 1930)
- Five US Amateur (1924, 1925, 1927, 1928, 1930)
- British Amateur (1930)

What else was he famous for?

- After retiring in 1930, Jones was responsible for founding the US Masters tournament.

- Jones developed the first set of matched clubs in the early 1930s. The Bobby Jones Golf Company continues to make golf clubs to this day.

Did you know?

- As a young boy plagued by ill health, Jones was prescribed golf to strengthen him.

- Jones is the only player to have won all four designated major tournaments in one calendar year. (The British and US Amateur titles were counted as majors at the time, alongside the British and US Open.)

- In 1958, Jones became only the second American to be named a Freeman of the City of St Andrews – the first being Benjamin Franklin in 1759 – a big change from his first appearance on the course, when he withdrew during the third round of the 1921 Open.

Sam Snead (1912–2002)

Nationality: American

Nickname: Slammin' Sam (due to the long drives for which he was famous)

Big wins:

- Open Championship (1946)
- Three US Masters (1949, 1952, 1954)
- Three US PGAs (1942, 1949, 1951)
- Snead never won the US Open, despite finishing second four times.

What else was he famous for? From 1984 until 2002, Snead hit the ceremonial, opening tee shot at the US Masters.

Did you know?

- Snead taught himself to play golf in the Virginian backwoods where he grew up, using clubs fashioned from tree branches.
- Snead became the youngest PGA-Tour player to shoot his age – 67 – in 1979.
- At the age of 71, Snead shot a 60 (12 under par) at The Homestead in Hot Springs, Virginia, where he first learnt his trade.
- Snead popularised the use of the sand wedge for lofted shots from grass.

Ben Hogan (1912–1997)

Nationality: American

Nickname: The Hawk, The Wee Ice Mon (bestowed after his Open victory at Carnoustie)

Big wins:

- Open Championship (1953)
- Four US Opens (1948, 1950, 1951, 1953)
- Two US Masters (1951, 1953)
- Two US PGAs (1946, 1948)

What else was he famous for?

- Hogan's golf-instruction book, *Five Lessons: The Modern Fundamentals of Golf*, is the best-selling book of its genre ever written.
- Hogan was in the US Air Force from 1943–1945.

Did you know?

- Hogan's father committed suicide when young Ben was just nine years of age.
- Hogan was the first golfer to seriously practise when away from the course.
- In his early golfing years, Hogan was so poor that he moonlighted as a croupier at a gambling den at Fort Worth.
- Hogan was nearly killed by a head-on collision with a Greyhound bus in thick fog in 1949. He didn't play golf for 11 months.

◉ THE POST-WAR TRIUMVIRATE ◉

Arnold Palmer

DOB: 10.9.29

Nationality: American

Nickname: The King

Big wins:

- Two Open Championships (1961, 1962)

- US Open (1960)

- Four US Masters (1958, 1960, 1962, 1964)

What else is he famous for?

- Palmer is a qualified pilot and set a world-flight record in 1976 by circumnavigating the globe in 57 hours, 25 minutes and 42 seconds.

- The Arnold Palmer Design Company was formed in 1972, after he negotiated a deal to build the first golf course in China.

- Palmer owns, and lives near, the Bay Hill Club and Lodge in Florida. The club hosts the annual Arnold Palmer Invitational on the PGA Tour.

- He underwent successful prostate-cancer surgery in 1997 and has since championed programmes supporting cancer research.

- He also has a drink named after him: a blend of iced tea and lemonade, sold widely in the USA.

Did you know?

- A charismatic performer, Palmer is credited with extending the popularity of golf as a spectator sport with the onset of television: his faithful fans were known as 'Arnie's army'.

- Prior to turning professional, Palmer served in the Coast Guard for three years.

- Palmer remains in the top 20 golf earners, despite not playing in major tournaments since 2004.

Gary Player

DOB: 1.11.35

Nationality: South African

Nickname: The Black Knight (due to his trademark-black playing attire)

Big wins:

- Three Open Championships (1959, 1968, 1974)
- US Open (1965)
- Three US Masters (1961, 1974, 1978)
- Two US PGAs (1962, 1972)

What else is he famous for?

- Player is an accomplished golf-course architect, with more than 300 designs across the world.
- His company, Black Knight International, covers a number of business ventures including licensing, clothing and publishing.
- The Player Foundation raises funds to enable the education of underprivileged children.

Did you know?

- Player is the son of a gold miner. His brother, Dr Ian Player, is a conservationist who saved the white rhino from extinction.
- Player has a passion for horse racing and owns a stud farm near Johannesburg.

Jack Nicklaus

DOB: 21.1.40

Nationality: American

Nickname: The Golden Bear

Big wins:

- Three Open Championships (1966, 1970, 1978)
- Four US Opens (1962, 1967, 1972, 1980)
- Six US Masters (1963, 1965, 1966, 1972, 1975, 1986)
- Five US PGAs (1963, 1971, 1973, 1975, 1980)

What else is he famous for?

- Nicklaus' golf-course-design company has 341 courses open for play in 34 countries.

- Nicklaus is honorary chairman of the Nicklaus Children's Health Care Foundation in Florida. The major fundraiser is 'The Jake', an annual pro-am golf tournament named in remembrance of his 17-month-old grandson, who drowned in a hot tub in 2005.

- Nicklaus owns Nicklaus Golf Equipment, which was founded in 1992.

Did you know?

- Nicklaus has earned more from his second career in golf-course design than from the professional golfing career that made his name.

- Nicklaus' flawless performance in winning the 1965 Masters by nine shots forced the Augusta National club to make changes to the course to make it tougher.

- In 1986, Nicklaus became the oldest winner of the US Masters in history, with an incredible last-round 65.

- There is a museum dedicated to Nicklaus in his home town of Columbus, Ohio.

Pocket Fact

Jack Nicklaus has won more major championships than any other player in history.

◉ MODERN GREATS ◉

Tom Watson

DOB: 4.9.49

Nationality: American

Nickname: Huckleberry Dillinger – in joint recognition of both his fresh face and his competitive attitude

Big wins:

- Five Open Championships (1975, 1977, 1980, 1982, 1983)
- US Open (1982)
- Two US Masters (1977, 1981)

What else is he famous for?

- Watson has become a respected golf-course designer, putting his name to many courses across the world.
- Watson helped raise over $3m (approx. £2.5m) for charities to fight ALS (also known as Lou Gehrig's Disease), which claimed the life of his long-time caddie in 2004.

Did you know?

- Watson nearly became the oldest major-championship winner in history when he defied his 59 years to tie for the lead at the end of the 2009 Open.
- Watson holds a degree in psychology.
- Watson has written an instructional column in *Golf Digest* magazine since the mid-1970s.

Pocket Fact

Jack Nicklaus finished second in half of Tom Watson's major wins.

Greg Norman

DOB: 10.2.55

Nationality: Australian

Nickname: The Great White Shark

Big wins:

- Two Open Championships (1986, 1993)
- US Open: 2nd (1984, 1995)

- US Masters: 2nd (1986, 1987, 1996)

- US PGA: 2nd (1986, 1993)

What else is he famous for? Norman's company, Great White Shark Enterprises, covers his extensive business interests – which range from golf fashion and course design to Wagyu beef (a marbled culinary delicacy) and wine estates.

Did you know?

- As a child, Norman's games were rugby and Australian rules football. He didn't spend much time playing golf until he was 15 and caddying for his mother – he would borrow her clubs after her round.

- Norman is almost as famous for his many 'near misses' as his wins: he is one of only two players to have competed in – and, like Craig Wood, to have lost – play-offs in all four of the major championships.

Severiano Ballesteros

DOB: 9.4.57

Nationality: Spanish

Nickname: Seve

Big wins:

- Three Open Championships (1979, 1984, 1988)

- Two US Masters (1980, 1983)

- Five World Match Play Championships

What else is he famous for? Since being diagnosed with a brain tumour in 2008, Seve has set up a foundation to help cancer sufferers and financially challenged, young golfers.

Did you know?

- Seve learned the game while playing on the beaches near his home, while he was supposed to be in school, mainly using a 3-iron given to him by one of his older brothers (all three of his brothers were also golf pros).

- Seve was the first-European player to win the US Masters.

- Together with Jose Maria Olazabal, Seve formed the most successful partnership in Ryder Cup history. The 'Spanish armada', as they were known, won 11 of their 15 matches together.

- On his way to his first Open title, Seve hit a tee shot into a car park . . . and still made birdie!

Sir Nick Faldo
DOB: 18.7.57

Nationality: English

Big wins:

- Three Open Championships (1987, 1990, 1992)
- Three US Masters (1989, 1990, 1996)

What else is he famous for? In 2009, Faldo became only the second golfer to be knighted (the first was Sir Henry Cotton).

Did you know?

- Faldo took up golf with borrowed clubs at the age of 13, after watching Jack Nicklaus play at the US Masters.

- Faldo is both the youngest and the most successful Ryder-Cup player – no one else on either team has amassed as many points.

Colin Montgomerie OBE
DOB: 23.6.63

Nationality: Scottish

Nickname: Monty

Big wins:

- Eight European Tour Order of Merit wins
- Has finished runner-up in five major championships

What else is he famous for?

- Monty established the Elizabeth Montgomerie Foundation to support lung cancer patients in Scotland, in memory of his mother.

- Monty has his own clothing range of knitwear and formal wear, with designs incorporating the Montgomerie Tartan.

Did you know?

- Monty's father, James, was managing director of Fox's Biscuits.

- Monty was selected as captain of the 2010 Ryder-Cup team.

- Colin Montgomerie's pre-shot routine includes reciting the 37-times table!

Ernie Els

DOB: 17.10.69

Nationality: South African

Nickname: The Big Easy

Big wins:

- Open Championship (2002)
- Two US Opens (1994, 1997)
- Seven World Match Play Championships

What else is he famous for?

- Els owns a winery in South Africa, which he started up in 1999 with a friend.

- Other interests include a golf-course-design business and a foundation in South Africa dedicated to helping underprivileged children play golf.

Did you know?

- Els has finished runner-up in six major championships.

- Since Els' son was diagnosed with autism, he and his wife have become involved in autism charities. This includes an annual, charity golf event, the Els for Autism Pro-Am, near his Florida residence.

Lee Westwood

DOB: 24.4.73

Nationality: English

Big wins:

- Open: 3rd (2009)
- US Open: 3rd (2008)
- US Masters: 2nd (2010)
- US PGA: 3rd (2009)
- Two European Tour Order of Merit wins (2000, 2009)

What else is he famous for? In 2009 Lee Westwood launched his Academy, a three-day training programme at various centres accross the UK, for boys and girls between the ages of 7 and 16.

Did you know? In 1997 Westwood postponed his wedding, scheduled for the week of the US Masters, when he learnt he had qualified for the tournament.

Eldrick Tont (Tiger) Woods

DOB: 30.12.75

Nationality: American

Nickname: Tiger

Big wins:

- Three Open Championships (2000, 2005, 2006)
- Three US Opens (2000, 2002, 2008)
- Four US Masters (1997, 2001, 2002, 2005)
- Four US PGAs (1999, 2000, 2006, 2007)

What else is he famous for?

- Woods rose to No. 1 on the Official Golf World Rankings in his 42nd week as a professional: the fastest-ever ascent.

- His 15-shot winning margin in the 2000 US Open was the largest in history.

Did you know?

- Woods' first golfing achievement was to beat comedian and avid golfer, Bob Hope, in a putting contest on the Mike Douglas Show on US national TV . . . at the age of two.

- He legally changed his name to Tiger on his 21st birthday.

- Prior to the recent well-documented problems in his personal life, Woods was the highest-earning sportsman in the world.

◎ WHO ARE THE MOST SUCCESSFUL ◎ GOLFERS?

The acid test of success for a professional golfer is whether they can win a major championship: this is how the greatest players in history made their reputations.

Most major championships won

- Jack Nicklaus: 18
- Tiger Woods: 14
- Walter Hagen: 11
- Ben Hogan: 9
- Gary Player: 9
- Tom Watson: 8
- Harry Vardon: 7
- Gene Sarazen: 7
- Bobby Jones: 7
- Sam Snead: 7

- Arnold Palmer: 7

- Nick Faldo: 6

- Lee Trevino: 6

However, majors do not always tell the whole story. Here are some of the best players in world golf who are yet to win a major:

- **Colin Montgomerie**. Won the European Order of Merit eight times, making him the richest player without a major. He also has five second-place major finishes.

- **Lee Westwood**. Recently finished 3rd, 3rd and 2nd in consecutive majors.

- **Sergio Garcia**. Two second-place major finishes.

- **Steve Stricker**. Currently a fixture in the world's top five.

- **Ian Poulter**. Finished 2nd in the 2008 Open.

- **Paul Casey**. Ranked as high as No. 3 in the world during 2009.

Pocket Fact

The Bank of Scotland issued a commemorative £5 note to mark Nicklaus' farewell appearance at the Old Course, St Andrews, making him only the third person to feature on a UK banknote during their lifetime, alongside Queen Elizabeth II and the Queen Mother.

Great amateur champions

1. **Walter J. Travis**. *Won the US Amateur Championship three times (1900, 1901, 1903), and by winning the British Amateur Championship in 1904, he became the first man to simultaneously hold both titles.*
2. **Jerome D. Travers**. *Won the US Amateur Championship four times (1907, 1908, 1912, 1913), and the US Open in 1915.*

3. **Francis Ouimet**. *Won the US Open in 1913, the first amateur to do so, and the US Amateur Championship in 1914 and 1931. His US Open victory – in a play-off against Harry Vardon and Ted Ray, two of the top professional golfers of the day – earned Ouimet a place in golf folklore.*

4. **Bobby Jones**. *Won the US Amateur Championship five times between 1924 and 1930 . . . when it was considered one of the majors.*

5. **Tiger Woods**. *Won the US Amateur Championship three times in succession between 1994 and 1996, before turning professional.*

◎ WOMEN IN GOLF ◎

HISTORY

While golf can often be perceived as a man's game, women have played a major part in its history from the very beginning, and have had their own championships for nearly as long as have men. Today, the LPGA professional circuit has 26 tournaments, just over half the number as on the men's PGA Tour – although they offer less than 20% of the prize money.

Women's golf landmarks

- **1567**: Mary Queen of Scots, reputed to be the first woman to play golf in Scotland, causes a scandal by playing days after her husband's murder.

- **1811**: The first all-women's golf championship is contested at Musselburgh Golf Club, Scotland.

- **1867**: St Andrews forms 'The Ladies' Club', the first golf club to create a women's golf organisation.

- **1893**: The Ladies' Golf Union is formed to sponsor the first British Ladies' Championship at Royal Lytham & St Annes, won by Lady Margaret Scott.

- **1895**: The first US Women's Amateur Golf Championship is played in New York. Thirteen players take part.

- **1932**: The first Curtis-Cup match (between US women amateur golfers and their British or Irish counterparts) is won by the US.

- **1945**: Babe Zaharias plays in three tournaments on the men's PGA Tour, making two of the three cuts.

- **1950**: The Ladies' Professional Golf Association (LPGA) is formed.

- **1964**: The first complete set of ladies' tees is designed at Crooked Stick Golf Club in Indianapolis.

- **1977**: The PGA accepts female members.

- **1996**: Karrie Webb becomes the first female golfer to earn over $1m in a season.

- **2001**: The current classification of major championships is adopted by the women's game.

- **2003**: Annika Sörenstam becomes the first woman to play in a men's PGA tournament in 58 years.

MAJOR WOMEN'S GOLF TOURNAMENTS

As in the men's game, women compete for four major championships. The championships counted as 'majors' have varied over the years, with the number set at four since 1983. Here is the current list:

- **Women's British Open**. This is the equivalent of the men's British Open, and, like the men's, has been rotated around leading courses in England and Scotland since it became a major championship in 2001.

- **US Women's Open**. This is the equivalent of the men's US Open, and has been part of the roster of majors since the LPGA's foundation in 1950.

- **LPGA Championship**. This is the equivalent of the men's PGA Championship. It began in 1955.

- **Kraft Nabisco Championship**. This has been one of the majors since 1983. The tournament is played at the Mission Hills Country Club course, and there is a tradition that the winner leaps into the lake at the 18th hole!

FAMOUS WOMEN GOLFERS

As with the men's game, the popularity of women's golf is driven by the characters playing the game. Here are some of golf's most famous women, both past and present.

(Note: because the classification of major tournaments has varied over time, the 'big wins' listed in this section are the tournaments counted as 'majors' in the years in question.)

Babe Zaharias (1911–1956)

Nickname: Babe (she was originally christened Mildred Ella Didrikson)

Nationality: American

Big wins:

- Three US Women's Opens (1948, 1950, 1954)
- Four Western Opens (1940, 1944, 1945, 1950)
- Three titleholders (1947, 1950, 1952)

Did you know?

- Zaharias excelled at many sports, and won two track and field gold medals in the 1932 Olympics.
- She also won a tournament at the 1931 State Fair of Texas: the sewing championship!
- Zaharias competed in numerous men's competitions and is the last woman to make the cut in a PGA tournament.

Mickey Wright

DOB: 14.2.35

Nickname: Mickey (she was originally christened Mary)

Nationality: American

Big wins:

- Four US Women's Opens (1958, 1959, 1961, 1964)
- Four LPGA Championships (1958, 1960, 1961, 1963)
- Three Western Opens (1962, 1963, 1966)
- Two titleholders (1961, 1962)

Did you know?

- In 1962 Wright became the only golfer to simultaneously hold all four majors – although her fourth title was in a different playing season, meaning that the women's Grand Slam (all four majors in the same playing season) is still to be completed.

- Wright was eventually forced to cut down her playing due to foot and wrist injuries, but still managed to get into a play-off at the Coca-Cola Classic in 1979 despite having to play in trainers.

Kathy Whitworth

DOB: 27.9.39

Nationality: American

Big wins:

- Three LPGA Championships (1967, 1971, 1975)
- Western Open (1967)
- Two titleholders (1965, 1966)

What else is she famous for?

- Whitworth was thrice president of the LPGA executive board, which directs the policies of the LPGA Tour.

- Whitworth is one of the most renowned female golf teachers.

Did you know?

- Whitworth won 88 tour championships – more than any other golfer.

- She was the first female golfer to amass $1m (approx. £687,000) in career earnings.

Annika Sörenstam

DOB: 9.10.70

Nationality: Swedish

Big wins:

- Women's British Open (2003)
- Three US Women's Opens (1995, 1996, 2006)
- Three LPGA Championships (2003, 2004, 2005)
- Three Kraft Nabisco Championships (2001, 2002, 2005)

What else is she famous for? Sörenstam has written an instructional book, which was released in 2004.

Did you know?

- Sörenstam hit the lowest round in LPGA-Tour history with a 59 in 2001.
- Golf runs in the Sörenstam family: her sister, Charlotta, also plays on the LPGA Tour.
- In 2003, Sörenstam competed in a PGA-Tour event, missing the cut but gaining in profile and popularity.

Karrie Webb

DOB: 21.12.74

Nationality: Australian

Big wins:

- Women's British Open (2002)
- Two US Women's Opens (2000, 2001)
- LPGA Championship (2001)
- Two Kraft Nabisco Championships (2000, 2006)
- du Maurier Classic (1999)

Did you know?

- In 1995, Webb played the LPGA qualifying tournament with a broken bone in her wrist . . . and still finished second.

- The following year, Webb became the first golfer to earn $1m in a single season of the LPGA Tour.

◉ JUNIOR GOLF ◉

Globally, golf is more highly developed at a junior level than ever before: approximately 9% of golf-club members in the UK and Ireland are juniors. Many foundations exist to facilitate the golfing prowess of young players.

JUNIOR TOURNAMENTS

The Callaway Junior World Golf Championship, held in the US every July, is guaranteed to attract the stars of the future, having previously been entered by the likes of Tiger Woods, Ernie Els, and Phil Mickelson. At a local level, the British Junior Golf Tour, which holds events across the UK throughout the year, is a good place to spot up-and-coming local talent.

GOLF'S BEST YOUNG PLAYERS

Here are some of the young players who are leading the field at the moment:

Rory McIlroy

DOB: 4.5.89

Nationality: Northern Irish

Big wins:

- 2009 Dubai Desert Classic

- Tied in 3rd position at the 2009 PGA Championship

Why will he succeed? He made the cut in all four major tournaments at his first attempt in 2009 – something even Tiger Woods failed to do in his first year.

Chris Wood

DOB: 26.11.87

Nationality: English

Big wins:

- Won the Silver Medal for 'Best Amateur', by finishing 5th at the 2008 Open Championship.

- Finished one shot off the play-offs in the 2009 Open.

Why will he succeed? He's a big hitter with a good all-round game, and was named the European Tour's rookie of the year in 2009.

Edoardo Francesco and Molinari

DOB: 11.2.81; 8.11.82

Nationality: Italian

Big wins:

- Francesco won the Italian Open in 2006, and has finished in the top 15 of both the British Open and US PGA.

- Edoardo set a new record for earnings on the Challenge Tour in 2009, securing entry into the 2010 European Tour.

Why will they succeed? Both have risen into the top 50 and are regularly competing in the major championships.

How to get started in junior golf
The Golf Foundation

The Golf Foundation, a charity set up to help young people develop 'Skills for Life' through golf, has Starter Centres (also known as 'Golf Roots Centres') across the UK, which offer beginners' courses at little or no cost. The Junior Golf Passport, a national learning programme, is set up to enable children to learn about golf through activities and fun, from a qualified PGA coach. It's a bit like a handicap system for children, as it

> *is a record of progress until your standard is high enough to warrant an official CONGU handicap.*
>
> **Get into Golf**
> *The English Golf Union (EGU) and the English Golf Women's Association (EGWA) have launched a scheme called 'Get Into Golf', which helps you find locally available resources, including free coaching schemes and how to start playing.*

⊚ CELEBRITY GOLFERS ⊚

Golf is traditionally the sport of choice for many of the rich and famous: some, like Clint Eastwood or Bill Gates, are members of exclusive clubs; while others, like Willie Nelson or Celine Dion, cut out the middleman by purchasing their own course! But who has the best celebrity-golf handicap?

LEADING CELEBRITY MALE GOLFERS

- **Kenny G (jazz saxophonist, USA)**. Current handicap: scratch – which means he plays to professional standard!

- **Ivan Lendl (tennis player, USA)**. Current handicap: scratch. Lendl has previously attempted to qualify for the US Open.

- **Samuel L. Jackson (actor, USA)**. Current handicap: 5. Has a putting green installed at home.

- **Alice Cooper (rock singer, USA)**. Current handicap: 7. Hosts an annual charity golf competition, and credits golf for helping him beat alcohol addiction: his autobiography was entitled *Alice Cooper, Golf Monster*.

- **Boris Becker (tennis player, Germany)**. Current handicap: 7. An enthusiastic participant in charity and pro-am tournaments.

- **Hugh Grant (actor, England)**. Current handicap: 7. A self-confessed 'golf tragic', often seen on the classic Scottish courses.

- **Jack Nicholson (actor, USA)**. Current handicap: 13. A familiar figure on the Hollywood golfing scene, Nicholson has a private driving range at home.

- **Clint Eastwood (actor, USA)**. Current handicap: 14. Owns Tehama Golf Club in California, and maintains close connections with Pebble Beach Golf Links.

- **Sean Connery (actor, Scotland)**. Current handicap: 22. Instigated one of the first British pro-am tournaments called The Sean Connery Invitational.

LEADING CELEBRITY FEMALE GOLFERS

- **Celine Dion (singer, Canada)**. Current handicap: 17. Owns a golf course.

- **Jodie Kidd (model and actress, England)**. Current handicap: 18. Kidd designs golf shoes and has birdied the Road Hole at St Andrews.

- **Belinda Carlisle (singer, USA)**. Current handicap: 23. Has been known to take golf lessons at Bel Air Country Club.

- **Catherine Zeta Jones (actress, Wales)**. Current handicap: 24. When prospective husband, Michael Douglas, learnt that Zeta Jones was an avid and accomplished amateur golfer, he said: 'That's it – the deal's done!'

- **Jane Seymour (actress, USA)**. Current handicap: 25. She once holed a bunker shot at the Northern Rock All-Star Cup.

Bing Crosby

The most influential celebrity golfer was singer, film star and tireless golfing enthusiast, Bing Crosby, who in 1937 organised the first major pro-am golf tournament: the 'Crosby Clambake', still played to this day as the AT&T Pebble Beach National Pro-Am. While Bing's original intention had been to instigate a gathering of friends as much as a tournament, the Clambake became immensely popular due to the star quality it

> *attracted. Bing was inducted into the World Golf Hall of Fame in 1978, the year after his death from a heart attack on the golf course. True to form, his last words were: 'That was a great game of golf, fellas!'*

PRESIDENTS AND PRIME MINISTERS

> *Golf is a game kings and presidents play when they get tired of running countries.*
> Charles Price

Golf has always been popular with those in high-political positions, with many 20th-century British Prime Ministers enjoying the game, including:

- **Arthur Balfour (Prime Minister 1902–1905)**. 'I am quite certain that there has never been a greater addition to the lighter side of civilisation than that supplied by the game of golf.'

- **David Lloyd George (Prime Minister 1916–1922)**. 'You get to know more of the character of a man in a round of golf than in six months of political experience.'

- **Winston Churchill (Prime Minister 1940–1945, 1951–1955)**. 'Golf is a game whose aim is to hit a very small ball into an even smaller hole, with weapons singularly ill-designed for the purpose.'

Pocket Fact

According to the North-Korean-government media, the country's leader, Kim Jong-Il, is the best golfer ever seen, having managed five holes in one in his first round to finish 38 shots under par!

The same is true across the Atlantic, where 15 of the last 18 US Presidents have sought the peace and quiet of the golf course:

- **Lyndon B. Johnson (President 1963–1969)**. 'I don't have any handicap. I am all handicap.'

- **Gerald Ford (President 1974–1977)**. 'I know I'm getting better at golf because I'm hitting fewer spectators. Either that, or fewer people are watching me play.'

- **Ronald Reagan (President 1981–1989)**. 'My golf-loving friend, Bob Hope, asked me what my handicap was, so I told him – Congress.'

- **George Bush Sr. (President 1989–1993)**. 'It's amazing how many people beat you at golf now that you're no longer President.'

- **George Bush Jr. (President 2001–2009)**. [Giving an interview on the golf course:] 'I call upon all nations to do everything they can to stop these terrorist killers. Thank you. Now watch this drive.'

Pocket Fact

Although perhaps the best golfer to occupy the White House, President Kennedy was careful never to be photographed on the golf course, as he had criticised his predecessor, Dwight Eisenhower, for playing too much!

6

A HOLE IN ONE: GOLF TOURS AND TOURNAMENTS

Whether it's a bet among friends or a $10m prize in the FedEx Cup, golf is driven by competition at all levels of the game. Many of the greatest legends on the world stage are defined by championship victories and near-misses, while the most prestigious tournaments have become the flagship events of the season. This chapter tells you all you need to know about golf as a competitive sport.

◉ DIFFERENT KINDS OF COMPETITION ◉

At amateur level, the prevalent form of competition is match play, a 'hole by hole' contest where the total number of strokes in the round is less important than the number of holes on which you beat your opponent. Here are the main types of match-play format you will come across:

SINGLES

This pits one player against another over a round of 18 holes. The aim is to take fewer shots than your opponent on each hole: if you do, you win the hole. If you get the same score, the hole is 'halved'. The match is won when one player leads by more holes than are remaining. If the match is level after 18 holes, play continues until there is a winner.

FOUR-BALL

Each team has two players, each of whom plays his or her own ball. As in singles, the competition is hole by hole, with the lower score of the two counting as the team's score for the hole. For example, if player A scores 4 and player B scores 3, the team would score 3. The team with the lower score wins the hole. If the match is level after 18 holes, play continues until there is a winner.

FOURSOMES

As in four-ball, this comprises two teams of two players, but there is only one ball per team with the players taking alternate shots. The team with the lower score wins the hole. This format is less common in everyday golf, but is played in the Ryder Cup. If the match is level after 18 holes, play continues until there is a winner.

◎ ENTERING AND WINNING ◎ A COMPETITION

With at least 50 million amateur golfers in the world, you will be able to find plenty of opportunities to pit your golfing skills against other players.

HOW TO SIGN UP

There are thousands of open golf competitions held annually in the UK, open to players of all standards. All you need is a current handicap, as this is how all of the different standards are accommodated. If you are a member of a club, it is usually advisable to start here where you will readily be able to find competition details. You are free to enter competitions elsewhere – however, these will have no handicap allowance, so your handicap needs to be close to scratch in order for you to be able to be competitive.

HOW TO WIN

As most amateur tournaments follow a match-play format, you will most often be drawn against another player and compete hole-by-hole for the better score, with the player who wins the most holes proceeding to the next round. The match is won when one player is leading by more holes than remain on the course.

If the match is tied, most competitions go into a 'sudden death' play-off.

PRIZES

At amateur level, the usual prize is a combination of money, a trophy or medal, and the satisfaction of winning but this varies by competition.

Pocket Fact

The most lucrative golf tournament in the USA or Europe is the FedEx Cup, with the winner pocketing a cool $10m (approx. £6.8m).

◎ FAMOUS TOURNAMENTS ◎

RYDER CUP

History: 'Officially' born in 1927, the Ryder Cup's origins lie in a pair of exhibition matches between the USA and Great Britain in 1921 and 1926. Samuel Ryder, a keen British golfer and business-man, who had made his wealth from selling penny seed packets, formalised the contest after watching the second game. The tour-nament has been played every two years since, interrupted only by the Second World War (1937–1947) and the terrorist attacks of 2001. In 1979, after an initial suggestion from Jack Nicklaus, the selection procedure was changed to allow European players to take part, which gave the competition a new lease of life as the USA had begun to dominate, retaining the Cup from 1959 to 1983.

Format: The present-day format was adopted in 1979, with four four-ball and four foursomes matches on each of the first two days, and 12 singles on the last day. One point is awarded for each match won, and half a point to each team if the match is halved, making 28 points available in total. The defending champions only need to halve the match itself (14 points each) to retain the trophy, but the challengers must win outright ($14\frac{1}{2}$ points or more).

Venue: The competition is held alternately in the USA and Europe.

Prize: The Cup itself is a gold trophy commissioned by Samuel Ryder in 1926. The players receive no payment for their involvement, as the associated prestige and gratitude of your country (or, in the case of Europe, continent!) are enough to attract the biggest stars.

Winners: USA 25 wins; GB/Europe 10 wins; two ties.

Did you know?

- GB/Europe have scored five holes in one, compared to the USA's one.

- It took the British team six days to travel to the first official competition.

Defining moment: The 1969 Ryder Cup was in the balance all the way to the last hole of the last match, between Jack Nicklaus and Tony Jacklin. Nicklaus holed out, leaving Jacklin a tricky three-footer to halve the match and the Cup . . . but, in a moment of supreme sportsmanship, Nicklaus picked up Jacklin's ball to concede the putt, sparing the British player the need to putt out and leaving the sides dead level.

Pocket Fact

The three-inch-high golfer on the top of the Ryder-Cup trophy was designed in the image of Abe Mitchell, one of the players in the British team of 1926.

US MASTERS

History: The first major tournament to be played each year, the Masters is also the newest of the four majors, established in 1934. The tournament was the brainchild of Bobby Jones, who designed the Augusta National course with famed golf-course architect, Dr Alister MacKenzie, and then inaugurated an annual, invitational tournament there. The Masters is still by invitation only, which means it has a smaller field of competitors than the other majors.

Format: Stroke play over four rounds of 18 holes each. After the first two rounds the field is reduced, with only players either within 44 places of the lead (including tied scores) or within 10 strokes of the leader retained. If there is a tie for first place at the end of the competition, there is a sudden-death play-off rotating between the 18th and 10th holes. 'Sudden death' means that the play-off is decided at the first hole where one player scores lower than the other.

Venue: Augusta National.

Prize: As well as the purse of $1.35m (approx. £920,000), the winner is awarded a green jacket (see box on page 114) and a gold medal; is granted honorary membership of Augusta National and a lifetime invitation to play the Masters; and is allowed to attend the Masters Club dinner for former champions, held every year on the Tuesday before the tournament. In addition, the player with the lowest score each day is presented with a crystal vase; and crystalware is also awarded in the event of a hole in one, albatross or eagle.

Winners:

- Six wins: Jack Nicklaus

- Four wins: Arnold Palmer, Tiger Woods

- Three wins: Jimmy Demaret, Gary Player, Sam Snead, Nick Faldo, Phil Mickelson

Did you know?

- The defending champion selects the menu for the Masters Club dinner, an opportunity that 1988-winner and proud Scotsman, Sandy Lyle, could not resist: that year, the 'Masters Club' dined on haggis.

- As befits a tournament established by an amateur golfer, the Masters traditionally supports amateur golfers by inviting winners of the major amateur tournaments, and pairing the current US Amateur champion with the defending Masters champion for the first two rounds.

Defining moment: In 1987, Augusta local, Larry Mize, took on the two best players of the moment, Seve Ballesteros and Greg Norman, in a play-off. After Ballesteros dropped out after the first hole, Mize missed the next green, but proceeded to hole his chip shot from 140 feet to stun Norman and win the most unlikely of Masters.

Pocket Fact

In 2010, Italian Matteo Manassero became the youngest Masters player to make the cut at 16 years of age, finishing as the leading amateur.

The Green Jacket

So famous that its colour is known simply as 'Masters Green', the distinctive Green Jacket was first worn by the club members at the 1937 Masters, to enable patrons to identify a reliable source of information. In 1949 came the first Green Jacket to be awarded to a Masters winner, Sam Snead. The following year, Snead returned and helped the next winner on with his own jacket, a tradition that continues to this day. Jack Nicklaus presented the club with a dilemma when he retained the championship in 1966, which they neatly solved by inviting him to put on his own coat. However, when Nick Faldo (1990) and Tiger Woods (2002) followed in Nicklaus' footsteps, it was the club chairman who assisted them into their Green Jackets. The winner can keep his jacket for the first year, after which it is returned to Augusta for him to wear whenever he returns.

Pocket Fact

Gary Player 'accidentally' took his Green Jacket back to South Africa with him after winning the 1961 Masters. He has never worn it in public, out of respect to the club.

UNITED STATES OPEN CHAMPIONSHIP (US OPEN)

History: The first US Open championship in 1895 attracted 11 players. The first native-born American didn't win until 1911, but the host nation has since made up for lost time, winning 84 of all subsequent tournaments! The tournament exploded in popularity during the 1920s, when Bobby Jones was at the height of his powers. Today, the US-Open is the second of the four major championships to be played each year.

Format: Stroke play over four rounds of 18 holes each. If there is a tie for first place at the end of the competition, the leaders play a fifth round of 18 holes on the following day. If this also ends level, there is a sudden-death play-off.

Venue: The venue is different every year, but the course is invariably challenging: few US-Open winners score significantly below the par score.

Prize: $1.35m (approx. £920,000). The winner is invited back to play the US Open for the next 10 years, and the other majors for the next five years.

Winners:

- Four wins: Willie Anderson, Bobby Jones, Ben Hogan, Jack Nicklaus.

Did you know?

- The first US Open took second billing to the first US Amateur championship, which took place on the same course in the same week.

- Willie Anderson is the only player to win the US Open in three successive years (1903–1905).

Defining moment: The 2008 Open ended in a tie between Tiger Woods and Rocco Mediate, forcing an 18-hole play-off the following day. After completing 90 holes over five days, both players were still tied, making only the third time in US Open history that a winner was determined using sudden death. On the first sudden-death hole (the 7th), Woods won the tournament with a par to defeat Mediate, who made a bogey. The victory made Woods the sixth player to win three or more US Opens.

Pocket Fact

In 1983, Forrest Fezler became the first player in US-Open history to wear shorts, when he changed in a portable toilet after the 17th hole in protest against the 'long trousers only' rule.

BRITISH OPEN CHAMPIONSHIP

History: The Open is the oldest national championship in golfing history. The first tournament was held in 1860 at Prestwick, and contested by just eight golfers from Scottish clubs. The following year, the invitation was extended to the rest of the world.

Format: The Open consists of four rounds of stroke play (see page 22). If there is a tie for the lead after four rounds, there is a four-hole play-off. If the scores are still level, the play-off becomes a 'sudden death' contest.

Venue: The tournament was rotated around the leading Scottish courses until 1894, when English clubs were included in the list for the first time. Today, nine courses in England and Scotland take it in turns to host the Open.

Prize: The original prize was a belt made of Moroccan leather with a silver buckle, with the rules stating that anyone who won the championship in three successive years would be allowed to keep the belt. However, the committee were so unprepared for Young Tom Morris' trio of victories from 1868–1870 that they cancelled the following year's tournament while they searched for a new prize! The famous Claret-Jug trophy has been presented every year since its introduction in 1872 – the committee having learnt from experience to keep it as their permanent property. The winner of the Open wins £800,000 plus a silver medal.

Winners:

- Six wins: Harry Vardon
- Five wins: James Braid, John Henry Taylor, Peter Thomson, Tom Watson
- Four wins: Walter Hagen, Bobby Locke, Old Tom Morris, Young Tom Morris, Willie Park Sr

Did you know?

- The runner-up at the 1863 Open, Old Tom Morris, earned more prize money than the winner, Willie Park! This is because Park enjoyed the accolade of being presented with the championship belt, while Morris shared £10 with the golfers in 3rd and 4th place.

- The Open is the only major championship to be held outside the US.

Defining moment: 1977's Duel in the Sun (see page 133).

Pocket Fact

Bobby Jones was the last amateur to win the tournament, in 1930.

PGA CHAMPIONSHIP

History: The PGA Championship is the last of the four majors played in the calendar year. The first championship was played in 1916, after the Professional Golfers' Association of America hatched the idea for an annual, national golf championship.

Format: The PGA Championship was originally a match-play competition, but was changed to stroke play in 1958. The format now consists of four rounds of 18 holes each, with a cut halfway through. In the event of a tie after 72 holes, the players enter a 3-hole play-off – the PGA was the first championship to dispense with the traditional 18-hole play-off format.

Venue: The tournament has been held at over 70 different courses, although in recent years it has been mostly rotated around a smaller group of notable venues, such as Oakland Hills Country Club and Medinah Country Club.

Prize: $1.35m (approx. £920,000). The winner is presented with the Wanamaker Trophy (named after the department-store mogul who originally donated it) gains a lifelong invitation to the PGA Championship; a five-year membership of the PGA Tour; and automatic participation in the other majors for the next five years.

Winners:

- Five wins: Walter Hagen, Jack Nicklaus

- Four wins: Tiger Woods

- Three wins: Gene Sarazen, Sam Snead

Did you know?

- The PGA Championship is the only major not to allow amateurs to compete unless they have won another of the major championships, thus gaining an automatic place in the field.

- The PGA Championship is the only major to have been won by the same player in four consecutive years. Walter Hagen achieved this feat from 1924–1927.

- Because of its position at the end of the season, the PGA Championship is known as 'Glory's Last Shot', and invariably attracts the strongest field of any competition.

Defining moment: Valhalla, 2000. Tiger Woods, looking to win his third-consecutive major, and outsider, Bob May, were tied after both making birdie putts on the 18th hole in the final round. Late in the afternoon they began the first three-hole, aggregate-score play-off in the tournament's history. Woods went ahead with a birdie on the 16th, then saved par on the final two holes with brilliant recovery shots to edge May by a stroke, with May narrowly missing his birdie attempt on the last hole. Woods called it 'one of the best duels in a major championship'.

Pocket Fact 🚩

Gene Sarazen holds the distinction of being both the tournament's youngest winner and its oldest player.

PRESIDENTS CUP

History: The Presidents Cup was first played in 1994. The contest involves a series of matches between a team representing the USA, and an 'International Team' made up of players from non-European countries, who are therefore ineligible for the Ryder Cup. The tournament is held in alternate years to the Ryder Cup.

Format: The format partially mirrors the Ryder Cup, with six matches of foursomes played on the Thursday, six of four-ball on the Friday, five of each on the Saturday and 12 singles matches on the Sunday.

Venue: The venue alternates between the USA and countries represented by the International Team.

Prize: There is no prize money for winning the Presidents' Cup: the proceeds are shared around charities nominated by the participants.

● **Winners**: USA six wins; International one win; one tie.

Did you know? The original format for settling a tied tournament was for the captains to select a team member to play a tie-breaker; the choice was only revealed in the event of a tie. However, this was discontinued after 2003, when darkness forced the abandonment of the tie-breaker and the team captains, Jack Nicklaus (USA) and Gary Player (International), agreed to share the Cup.

Pocket Fact 🚩

The 2011 tournament takes place at the Royal Melbourne Golf Club, of which the International Team captain, Greg Norman, is a member.

SENIOR PGA CHAMPIONSHIP

What's nice about our tour is you can't remember your bad shots.
Bob Bruce

History: Founded in 1937, the Senior PGA was the first 'major' tournament held exclusively for senior golfers. Like the Masters, the Senior PGA is indebted to Bobby Jones, who organised the championship and suggested that the inaugural tournament be held at Augusta National Golf Club.

Format: The tournament is open to all golfers of the required standard, over 50 years of age.

Venue: Although the tournament was staged at the PGA National Golf Club in Florida from 1982–2000, it now rotates around different venues each year, like the PGA Championship.

Prize: The winner pockets $360,000 (approx. £247,000), and is presented with the Alfred S. Bourne trophy. Bourne, one of the original members of Augusta National, paid for the trophy to be made. The winner also gains entry into the PGA Championship later in the season.

Winners:

- Six wins: Sam Snead
- Four wins: Hale Irwin
- Three wins: Eddie Williams, Al Watrous, Gary Player

◎ PROFESSIONAL MEN'S GOLF TOURS ◎

A 'tour', in golfing terms, is a series of separate tournaments, organised into a unified schedule by a governing body. There are over twenty professional golf tours in operation, each with its own card-carrying members. The status of a tour is usually connected to the financial rewards it offers: on this basis, the PGA and European Tours are at the pinnacle of the game.

TOURNAMENTS INCLUDED IN BOTH LEADING TOURS (AS OF 2009)

The four major championships and the four World Golf Championships are counted in both the PGA and the European Tours. However, the major tournaments are no longer the most lucrative in terms of total prize money:

- World Golf Championships – Accenture Match Play Championship: $8.5m (approx. £5.8m)

- World Golf Championships – CA Championship: $8.5m (approx. £5.8m)

- World Golf Championships – Bridgestone Invitational: $8.5m (approx. £5.8m)

- US Masters: $7.5m (approx. £5.1m)

- US Open: $7.5m (approx. £5.1m)

- US PGA: $7.5m (approx. £5.1m)

- Open Championship: $7m (approx. £4.8m)

- World Golf Championships – HSBC Champions: $7m (approx. £4.8m)

THE PROFESSIONAL GOLFERS' ASSOCIATION (PGA) TOUR

The foremost golf tour in the world, in terms of prize money and elite golfers, the PGA Tour is based in Florida and stages all but a handful of its tournaments in the USA. The current tour schedule consists of 55 tournaments from January to November (including those shared with the European Tour), culminating in four 'play-off' tournaments for the top-125 points-scorers, who are gradually whittled down to 30 by the time of the 4th play-off: The Tour Championship. The highest points-scorer at the end of the play-offs wins the lucrative FedEx Cup.

Biggest prize money pots on the PGA Tour (as of 2009 – excluding shared tournaments):

- FedEx Cup: $35m (approx. £24m). The player with the most points from the PGA Tour (including the four play-off events) collects $10m, with the remainder allocated in diminishing amounts to all participants in the four play-off tournaments, plus the next 25 players who did not qualify for the play-offs.

- The Players Championship: $9.5m (approx. £6.5m). This is sometimes referred to as the 'Fifth Major', although it does not have major status and is not an official event on the European Tour.

- Play-off 1 – The Barclays Classic: $7.5m (approx. £5.1m)

- Play-off 2 – Deutsche Bank Championship: $7.5m (approx. £5.1m)

- Play-off 3 – BMW Championship: $7.5m (approx. £5.1m)

- Play-off 4 – THE TOUR Championship presented by Coca-Cola: $7.5m (approx. £5.1m)

THE PGA EUROPEAN TOUR

Second only to the PGA Tour in terms of worldwide prestige, the European Tour was introduced in 1972. Its headquarters are at Wentworth Golf Club. Most of the tournaments are held in Europe, although an increasing number are held in non-European countries. Partly because of the danger that players on the European Tour will 'defect' to the more lucrative PGA Tour, the European Tour has recently added the three USA major championships – the Masters, the US Open and the PGA Championship – to its official itinerary, followed by the World Golf Championships. The 2010 season includes 49 separate tournaments (including those shared with the PGA Tour) from December to November.

Biggest prize money pots on the European Tour (2009 – excluding shared tournaments):

- Dubai World Championship: $7.5m (approx. £5.1m)
- BMW PGA Championship: €4.5m (approx. £3.8m)
- Alfred Dunhill Links Championship: $5m (approx. £3.4m)
- Barclays Scottish Open: £3m
- Alstom Open de France: €3m (approx. £2.5m)
- 3 Irish Open: €3m (approx. £2.5m)
- Portugal Masters: €3m (approx. £2.5m)
- Andalucia Masters: €3m (approx. £2.5m)

Touring Professionals

Only a small proportion of professional golfers earn their living from playing on the tournament circuit: these are also known as 'touring professionals'. Of these, an even smaller number make a lucrative income from the game. Playing on a professional golf tour can be expensive once the following costs are factored in:

- Travelling from course to course
- Accommodation
- Caddie hire or employment
- Possibility of earning nothing: only players who 'make the cut' are included in the prize-money allocation

⦿ TOURNAMENTS FOR WOMEN ⦿

LPGA CHAMPIONSHIP

History: The second major of the season, the LPGA Championship was first played in 1955 – five years after the LPGA Tour was founded.

Format: The first tournament combined three rounds of stroke play with a final round of match play, but this was scrapped the following year in favour of four 18-hole rounds of stroke play. The LPGA Championship is open to professional golfers only.

Venue: Many different courses have hosted the Championship, most recently Locust Hill Country Club in New York.

Prize: The winner receives $300,000 (approx. £206,000)

Winners:

- Four wins: Mickey Wright
- Three wins: Kathy Whitworth, Nancy Lopez, Patty Sheehan, Se Ri Pak, Annika Sörenstam

Did you know? The 'professionals only' rule was revoked in 2005 for one year only, in order to allow the accomplished amateur golfer, Michelle Wie, to compete.

Pocket Fact 🚩

Over 100,000 spectators attend the LPGA Championship every year.

KRAFT NABISCO CHAMPIONSHIP

History: The tournament began in 1972, and has been classified as one of the majors since 1983.

Format: The first tournament consisted of three 18-hole rounds of stroke play, later increased to four rounds.

Venue: The tournament is played at the Dinah Shore Tournament Course at Mission Hills Country Club in California.

Prize: The winner receives $300,000 (approx. £206,000)

Winners:

- Three wins: Amy Alcott, Betsy King, Annika Sörenstam
- Two wins: Julie Inkster, Dottie Pepper, Karrie Webb

Did you know? In 1982, the Kraft Nabisco Championship became the first LPGA tournament to be broadcast in full on national USA television.

Pocket Fact

An earthquake 90 miles away, measuring 7.2 on the Richter scale, rocked the 2010 championship – but only after play had finished.

Ladies of the Lake

The 18th hole at Mission Hills Country Club, the venue for the Kraft Nabisco Championship, boasts a lake that is more closely involved in the spectacle than most: there is a tradition that the winner takes a victory leap into the water! The first player to take the plunge was Amy Alcott in 1988 after she was overcome by emotion upon winning. Alcott jumped in again after her third and final win in 1991, famously accompanied by tournament founder, Dinah Shore, and there have been many famous variations in the years since:

- *Lorena Ochoa's pool party in 2008, complete with a live mariachi band, set the record for the most people in the lake.*
- *Pat Hurst stuck to paddling when she won in 1998 – because she can't swim.*
- *Dottie Pepper didn't jump in at all after winning in a play-off in 1992, because the play-off finished on the 10th hole, not the 18th.*

Pocket Fact

In 2000, Karrie Webb was joined in her winning plunge by pop star, Celine Dion.

WOMEN'S BRITISH OPEN CHAMPIONSHIP

History: Although originally founded in 1976, the Women's British Open was only designated a major championship in 2001, replacing the du Maurier Classic.

Format: There are four 18-hole rounds of stroke play.

Venue: In its early years, the Open was hosted by the best clubs not in the rotation of the men's tournament; in particular, Woburn Golf & Country Club hosted for 10 consecutive years between 1987 and 1996. With its recent increase in profile and prestige, the Open is now also hosted by courses in the men's rotation, such as Royal Birkdale in 2010.

Prize: The winner receives £230,000 (approx. $335,000)

Winners:

- Three wins: Karrie Webb, Sherri Steinhauer
- Two wins: Debbie Massey

Did you know? In winning the 2009 Open, Scotland's Catriona Matthew secured her first major championship just 11 weeks after giving birth to her second child.

Pocket Fact

Three amateurs have won the British Open — the first, Jenny Lee-Smith, doing so in its inaugural year.

WOMEN'S US OPEN

History: The US Open was the first of the current majors to be designated as such, having first been played in 1946 and classed as a major in 1953. In terms of prize money, seniority and prestige, the US Open is the foremost of the women's golf majors.

Format: The first tournament was match play, but this was changed to stroke play the following year and has remained the format ever since. As in the other majors, there are four 18-hole rounds.

At the halfway point, the field is cut to 60 plus anyone within 10 strokes of the leader.

Venue: The tournament is played at a different venue every year.

Prize: The winner receives $585,000 (approx. £403,000)

Winners:

- Four wins: Betsy Rawls, Mickey Wright
- Three wins: Babe Zaharias, Susie Berning, Hollis Stacy, Annika Sörenstam

Did you know? In 1967, Beverly Klass became the youngest player to compete in the US Open, at just 10 years of age.

SOLHEIM CUP

History: Since 1990, the Solheim Cup has been contested by the USA and Europe. As the women's equivalent of the Ryder Cup, it is played in alternate years to the men's competition. The event is named after Norwegian-American golf club inventor, Karsten Solheim, who was instrumental in its creation.

Format: The match-play format of the Solheim Cup, comprising a mixture of foursomes, four-ball and singles, is the same as the Ryder Cup. The players are selected based primarily on rankings, with the team captains allowed to select a number of players at their own discretion.

Venue: The location of the Cup alternates between Europe and the USA, and has included such notable courses as Halmstad and Loch Lomond.

Prize: The Solheim Cup itself is an elaborate, glass construction valued at more than $50,000 (approx. £35,000)

Winners: USA eight wins; Europe three wins.

Did you know? There is also a 'junior' version of the Solheim Cup, for the best-performing amateur girls in the USA and Europe.

Pocket Fact 📍

Karsten Solheim made his fortune by creating Ping golf clubs. The brand was so named because of the sound Solheim's first putter made when it hit the ball.

OTHER WOMEN'S TOURNAMENTS

There are many other lucrative women's tournaments beside the four majors:

- Evian Masters: $3.25m (approx. £2.24m)
- Canadian Women's Open: $2.25m (approx. £1.5m)
- P&G NW Arkansas Championship presented by Walmart: $2m (approx. £1.3m)
- Sime Darby LPGA Malaysia: $1.8m (approx. £1.2m)
- LPGA Hana Bank Championship: $1.8m (approx. £1.2m)
- Kia Classic: $1.7m (approx. £1.1m)
- LPGA State Farm Classic: $1.7m (approx. £1.1m)
- Sybase Match Play Championship: $1.5m (approx. £1m)
- ShopRite LPGA Classic: $1.5m (approx. £1m)
- Safeway Classic presented by Coca-Cola: $1.5m (approx. £1m)

◉ AMATEUR TOURNAMENTS ◉

WALKER CUP

History: The Walker Cup is contested between the leading amateur golfers of the USA and Great Britain. The tournament was first played in 1922 as a means of generating interest in the sport, and has been played biennially in odd-numbered years since the Second World War.

Format: The present-day format was adopted in 1979. Four foursomes matches are played on each of the Cup's two mornings, with eight singles matches on the first afternoon and 10 on the second. One point is awarded for each match won, and half a point to each team if the match is halved, making 26 points available in total. The defending champions only need to halve the competition (13 points) to retain the Cup, but the challengers must win outright ($13\frac{1}{2}$ points minimum).

Venue: The competition is held alternately in the USA and Europe.

Prize: The Walker Cup is named after George Herbert Walker, who was president of the USGA when the competition came into being and agreed to donate the trophy.

Winners: US 34 wins; Great Britain seven wins; one tie.

Did you know?

- Walker is the great-grandfather of the former USA President, George W. Bush.

- The USA originally invited all nations to compete for the Walker Cup, but Great Britain was the only country able to meet the challenge.

CURTIS CUP

History: First played in 1932, the Curtis Cup is women's golf's equivalent of the Walker Cup, played biennially between amateur teams representing the USA and Great Britain. The original impetus came from the Curtis sisters, Harriot and Margaret, both of whom were prizewinning amateur golfers who donated the Cup itself.

Format: The two teams of eight compete in the main, different forms of match play – singles, foursomes and four-ball. Currently the competition is held over three days, with three foursomes and three four-ball matches on each of the first two days, and eight singles matches on the final day. Each match is worth one point, with half a point each if the match is tied after 18 holes. If the whole competition ends in a tie, the team defending the trophy is allowed to retain it.

Venue: The competition is held alternately in the USA and Europe.

Prize: Officially named the 'Women's International Cup', the trophy was designed by Paul Revere. An inscription on the side reads: 'To stimulate friendly rivalry among the women golfers of many lands.'

Winners: USA 27 wins; Great Britain six wins; three ties.

Did you know?

- The Curtis sisters were famous for their philanthropy as well as their golf: Margaret was awarded the Medaille de Guerre from the French Red Cross for her relief efforts during the First World War.

- Michelle Wie became the youngest player in Curtis-Cup history in 2004, winning both her singles matches at the age of 14.

PRESIDENTS' PUTTER

History: Ever since 1920, members of the Oxford & Cambridge Golfing Society have competed against each other during the first week of January. The Society comprises former undergraduates who represented the two venerable universities at golf, who are known as 'blues'. There is no age limit, so the age of the participants varies from 20 to 70.

Format: Match play between individuals.

Venue: Rye Golf Club, East Sussex.

Prize: The winner is given a silver medal in return for his winning ball.

Did you know?

- The oldest competitor was Peter Gracey, a parachutist during the Second World War, who played his last Putter aged 84!

- Former England cricketer, Ted Dexter, won the Putter twice in the 1980s.

SUNNINGDALE FOURSOMES

History: First played in 1934, the tournament is one of the first events in the golfing calendar, taking place in March.

Any combination of player may pair up – whether male or female, old or young, professional or amateur. Handicap levels for amateurs ensure the playing field remains level.

Format: Foursomes – some of the world's top amateurs hit alternate shots with professionals.

Venue: Sunningdale Golf Club (Surrey, England). Both the Old and New Courses are used.

Prize: If the winners are professionals, they receive a cash prize. Amateur players receive a gift voucher.

Did you know? Admission is free if you want to go and watch.

Attending a major tournament
How do I get tickets?
There's plenty of opportunities to see the Open Championship in person: the average Open draws crowds of at least 200,000 over the four days of play. It is advisable to purchase tickets from the R&A well in advance, especially if you want a seat in a grandstand. US-PGA-Championship tickets can also be purchased online. However, if you want to see the US Open, you need to enter a lottery by filling out an application form (available online). It is extremely difficult to secure tickets for the US Masters, as the waiting list was closed years ago.

How much does it cost?
The price of a basic, day ticket for the 2010 Open Championship was £60, with concessions for under-21s and over-65s. The US PGA Championship and US Open both cost between $95 and $110 (£75–£95) for basic admission; however, a tournament badge for the US Masters can set you back thousands of dollars.

◎ ALL-TIME GREATEST . . . ◎

WINS

- **Hogan's miracle victory (1950)**. In 1949, Ben Hogan had been involved in a head-on collision with a coach from which he was lucky to escape with his life. Sixteen months later, he still found walking uncomfortable, and the last day of the 50th US Open was the first time he had attempted to play 36 holes in a single day since his return. Not only did Hogan get round the course in extreme pain, he found the will to play a stunning 1-iron shot 200 yards onto the final green to force the match-winning play-off. A plaque on the fairway marks the spot where he hit the shot.

- **Nicklaus' first major win (1962)**. In his first year as a professional, Jack Nicklaus, 22, won the US Open by beating the reigning 'king of golf' and defending US Open champion, Arnold Palmer, in his own back yard – Oakmont was only 40 miles from Palmer's home, and the crowd was unashamedly partisan, cruelly christening Nicklaus: 'Ohio Fats'. The championship was decided by an 18-hole play-off after both players had narrowly missed birdie putts on the 72nd hole. Nicklaus led the play-off from the first hole to the last, and ended up defeating Palmer by three shots, having not only out-driven Palmer but also out-putted him.

- **Duel in the sun (1977)**. For two days, Tom Watson and Jack Nicklaus played their own private contest to decide the Open, finishing 10 shots ahead of the nearest competitor, Hubert Green, who remarked ruefully, 'I won the tournament I played in.' Nicklaus shot 65 and 66 in the last two rounds, only to lose by a single stroke. Even on the last, one shot down to Watson and trapped under a gorse bush off the tee, Nicklaus hit an amazing recovery shot onto the green and sunk the 40-foot putt for birdie, only for Watson to make a birdie himself to take the title. The spirit of the occasion was summed up when, on the 16th tee of the final round, Watson paused to say to Nicklaus: 'This is what it's all about, isn't it?'

- **Seve wins his first Open (1979)**. Three years after his second-place Open tie with Jack Nicklaus as a fresh-faced 19-year-old, Seve Ballesteros left Nicklaus three shots adrift with his first major win. It opened the floodgates for an influx of continental talent, which gathered momentum later that year when golfers from Europe competed in the Ryder Cup for the first time. The young Spaniard was initially branded the 'car park champion' after being forced to play a shot from a temporary car park near the 16th fairway. Typical of Ballesteros, he hit a spectacular recovery onto the green and sank the 30-foot birdie putt – the sort of cavalier playing style for which he became famous.

- **Seve becomes the first-European US Masters winner (1980)**. Starting with a first-round 66, six shots under par, Seve's golf was so good throughout the four rounds that he could even afford to lose seven shots in his final visit to Amen Corner and still finish four shots clear. He even found an escapade to rival the 'car park' incident: a wild tee shot on the par-4 17th landed on the 7th green, yet he managed to slam a blind iron shot onto the green and hole the putt for a birdie! In his own words: 'Drive fairway all the time, no fun. Make big hook, cause excitement.'

- **The Golden Bear rolls back the years (1986)**. At the age of 46, having been written off by all the experts, Jack Nicklaus stormed into the record books as the oldest champion in Masters history with a final round of 65, playing the daunting back nine in 30 to win by one shot from Tom Kite and Greg Norman. It was a feat that was as emotional as it was unexpected, and marked a full circle from Nicklaus' first major (see above).

- **The first-British Masters winner (1988)**. Scotsman, Sandy Lyle, teed off on the last hole, needing a birdie to win by one stroke, or a par to force a play-off with American, Mark Calcavecchia. When his tee shot flew into the first of the left fairway bunkers, even the play-off looked unlikely – but Lyle unleashed a towering 7-iron from the bunker that soared over the bunkers guarding the front of the green, landed past the flag, and trickled back to around 10 feet. He rolled in the birdie putt to become the first-British player to don the green jacket.

- **Tiger destroys the competition (1997)**. Woods won his first major in style, finishing 18 under par, 12 strokes beyond the rest of the field, to become the Masters' youngest-ever winner. It was an unprecedented performance, especially from a player who'd only turned professional eight months earlier, and demonstrated that golf – and the Augusta National course – would never be quite the same again.

Pocket Fact ⚑

Golf is the only sport to have been played on the surface of the moon. In 1971, the Apollo-14 astronaut, Alan Shepard, hit two golf balls with a makeshift golf club after smuggling the head of a 6-iron aboard in his spacesuit.

LOSSES

- **Palmer shows he is human (1966)**. As Arnold Palmer and Billy Casper reached the turn (the middle of the round) on the last day of the US Open at the Olympic Club's Lake Course, Palmer enjoyed a seemingly unassailable seven-shot lead, and was still five in front with four to play. But Casper made up all five strokes on the next three holes to force an 18-hole play-off the next day. Amazingly, history repeated itself: although Palmer again led going into the back nine, a six-shot swing over the last eight holes gave Casper the title.

- **Three feet from victory (1970)**. Doug Sanders stood on the final green at St Andrews, one shot ahead of Jack Nicklaus, with a 30-inch putt to win the Open – a formality on any other occasion. However, the putt was left to right and downhill, and the stakes were high. To gasps from the massed crowd, the putt dribbled to the right, and Sanders went on to lose the next day's 18-hole play-off by a single stroke. When asked if the experience had had a lasting effect on him, Sanders has said: 'No — some days I can go 20 minutes without thinking about it.'

- **Tom Watson lets a five-shot lead slip (1978)**. Watson was five shots clear of the field in the final round of the PGA Championship, only to end up tied with John Mahaffey and Jerry Pate. Mahaffey won the subsequent play-off; the PGA Championship was the only major to elude Watson.

- **Hoch, as in 'choke' (1989)**. Scott Hoch had already missed a 4-foot par putt on the 17th hole, which had reduced him to a sudden-death play-off against Nick Faldo. Faldo hit a bogey 5 on the first play-off hole, and Hoch was left with a 30-inch par putt to win the Masters . . . but the ball slid past the left of the hole. Faldo sank a 25-foot birdie putt to win his first Masters title at the very next hole. 'I'm glad I don't carry a gun with me,' Hoch said afterwards.

- **Norman's darkest hour (1996)**. Greg Norman began the final round of the Masters, six shots ahead of his nearest rival, Nick Faldo, who was paired with him in the final group. The round was expected to be a well-earned victory parade for Norman, who had lost a sudden-death Masters play-off in 1987, but it turned into one of the most spectacular collapses in golf history: Norman found water, hooked drives and missed putts to finish with a 78 — five behind Faldo, who hugged him almost apologetically after finishing with a birdie on the last for another unlikely Masters win.

- **Jean Van de Velde gets his feet wet (1999)**. Jean Van de Velde, a little-known French golfer, only needed a six on the final hole to win the Open at Carnoustie. With the infamous Barry Burn flowing across the fairway, the conservative option would have been to play short and leave a comfortable pitch to the green — but Van de Velde, refusing to compromise his attacking approach, went for the hole, only to hit his ball against the grandstand into thick rough. The next shot plummeted straight into the water, followed shortly afterwards by Van de Velde himself — minus his socks and shoes! Incredibly, after a drop, a further pitch into a bunker and subsequent recovery, Van de Velde had to hole a 6-foot putt just to get into a play-off, which was won by a grateful Paul Lawrie.

- **Mickelson is driven to distraction (2006)**. Standing on the 18th tee in the final round, Phil Mickelson needed only a par to win the US Open, but inexplicably decided to gamble by using the driver which had been misfiring all day: even on the 17th hole he had hit his tee shot into a dustbin. This time the result was even worse: the tee shot bounced off a hospitality tent, leaving his ball surrounded by trees. Again, he tried to go for glory instead of a safer, sideways shot, only for his ball to rebound off a tree and advance less than 50 yards. His next shot reached the green . . . but landed in a bunker at the back of the green. The result: a double-bogey and a one-shot win for Geoff Ogilvy. In Mickelson's own inimitable words: 'I am such an idiot.'

7

GETTING TO GRIPS WITH GOLF: YOUR GAME

Although the best players make golf look like a simple game, in reality it can be highly complex – for example, some golf instructors have split the humble swing into 14 separate stages! This chapter gives you a head start, with some of the most important hints and tips to improve all aspects of your golf game.

◎ WHY PLAY GOLF? ◎

There are many reasons why golf is one of the most widely played sports in the world. As well as simple enjoyment, there are a number of other benefits enjoyed by those who take up the sport.

HEALTH BENEFITS

> *Golf is a good walk spoiled.*
> Mark Twain

Did you know that playing golf is good for your health? One hour's exercise playing golf is estimated to burn 200–400 calories, depending on whether or not you walk all the way and carry your own clubs: this compares favourably with sports such as darts, snooker and bowling, or a short fitness class. This is because progress round an average course can represent up to four miles of walking – and the good news for beginners is that the worse your golf is, the further you are likely to walk!

SOCIAL ASPECTS

> *If you think it's hard to meet new people, try picking up the wrong golf ball.*
> Jack Lemmon

As a round of golf takes three or four hours, the game is much more enjoyable if you get on with your playing partners! For many, a big part of the attraction of golf is being able to spend time with your mates – and even if you don't know any golfers, a golf course is the perfect place to get to know new people. This is illustrated by the prevalence of golf clubs, even though the game itself is essentially a solo pastime. If you have a group of friends who all play golf, a golfing trip can be a great way to bond while experiencing some different courses and all the excitement of a holiday.

GOLF AS A BUSINESS TOOL

Golf and business have gone hand in hand since the game's popularity spiralled in the early 20th century. Today, nine out of 10 CEOs of Fortune-500 companies (the 500 largest companies in the USA) play golf, and most see the game as a business-development tool. Here are some of the major dos and don'ts if you play golf with a business colleague:

- **Getting to the course**. If you are extending the invitation, make sure your playing partner knows how to get to the course, and that they are familiar with key club rules, such as dress code.

- **Arrive early**. As well as giving the right first impression, this will put all parties at their ease, especially as golf clubs are sticklers for punctuality. If you are going to a new club, it will also allow you to get the 'lie of the land'; and even if you are familiar with the club, to check in and maybe purchase some practice balls from the club shop.

- **Never cheat**. Your behaviour on the golf course may be taken to reflect your character in life. However, keep a close eye on what your playing companions are doing: a recent US survey found that 82% of business executives cheat at golf! If you notice cheating, let it pass – an accusation, no matter how well founded, will only sour the mood.

- **Betting on the outcome**. Many top executives are competitive in all aspects of life. If you are asked to bet on the round, make sure the rules are clear in advance. If you lose, don't be a poor loser: consider the money an investment in the relationship.

- **The 19th hole** (see page 20). Make sure you buy the first round. If you want to talk business, do it as subtly as possible.

◎ PSYCHOLOGICAL ASPECTS ◎ OF PLAYING

Competitive golf is played mainly on a five-and-a-half-inch course – the space between your ears.
Bobby Jones

IMPORTANCE OF CONFIDENCE

More than many sports, golf is a confidence game, since there is no direct competitive input into your stroke: you are hitting a stationary ball on a pre-set course, with as much time as you require to plan and execute your shot. This can be either a blessing or a curse, as your frame of mind is vital to your golf game – the more confident you are in your game, the more successful you will be on the golf course.

Pocket Fact

More than 90% of your time on the golf course is spent in-between shots.

GETTING INTO THE ZONE

- **Don't let mistakes get to you**. One of the main problems affecting concentration is thinking about shots you've already played, and what you could have done differently – this will not help the mental side of your game. You should put any residual anger or annoyance out of your mind, in order to think exclusively about the upcoming shot.

- **Don't think about the score you want**. If you play a hole thinking 'I want a 4' then you will put yourself in danger of bad decision making or shot selection. Think about what shot you want to play next, and the score will take care of itself.

- **Develop a pre-shot routine**. If you watch professional players get ready before a shot, you will notice that they repeat the same mannerisms each time. This is because a routine before the shot helps them mentally focus on what they are doing, by eliminating irrelevant thoughts or behaviour. It doesn't matter what your routine is, although it helps if the routine covers both thoughts and actions. Some players will run through a certain number of practice swings, while others will place their hands on the club in the same way each time. Ultimately, you should stick to whatever works for you, as each golfer's pre-shot routine is unique.

- **Know what shot you want to play**. Some golfers, like Jack Nicklaus, start by creating a mental picture of what the shot they want to hit looks like, then a picture of themselves hitting that shot. Others make the shot 'real' in their mind by gauging the distance to the hole, the hazards in the way and the strength and direction of the wind, to decide where their ball should be hit. Either way, the key is to know what shot you want to play.

- **Think positively about your shot**. Once again, confidence is the key: if you are uncertain whether you have chosen the correct club, or the right line, the likelihood is that your shot will suffer. Make sure you are committed to your choice of shot before you start your pre-shot routine, and think about making the shot rather than failing at it.

- **Learn to switch on and off**. If you are focused on your game for the entire duration of the round, you are probably concentrating too hard. The best way to keep your intensity throughout the round is to 'switch off' once you have played your shot, and 'switch on' again when the time comes to prepare for the next one.

- **Learn from your experiences**. If you understand where you could have done better on the course, then you will not make that mistake again.

Pocket Caddie

Take a relaxed breath in and out before you take your shot, then swing the club before the next 'in' breath.

Keeping your temper

When I played, I never lost my temper. Sometimes, it is true, I may, after missing a shot, have broken my club across my knees; but I did it in a calm and judicial spirit, because the club was obviously no good and I was going to get another one anyway.

P.G. Wodehouse

Golf is a game that requires a temperate disposition and an ability to forget what went before. However, this is easier said than done – even the best players can 'lose it' occasionally. Here are some of the most famous examples:

- **'Terrible' Tommy Bolt**. *Although he won the US Open in 1958, Bolt was more famous for his explosions of temper on the golf course. His advice to golfers with a short fuse: 'Always throw clubs ahead of you – that way you won't waste any energy going back to pick them up.'*

- **Bobby Jones**. *Although in later years he became something of an ambassador for the sport, Jones was a young firebrand in his early years. His first visit to St Andrews in 1921 ended abruptly when he picked his ball up and walked off the 11th after landing in a bunker.*

- **Ben Crenshaw**. *Crenshaw, winner of two major championships, once snapped his putter in anger during a Ryder-Cup singles match, and had to putt for the remainder of the match with his 1-iron and sand wedge.*

- **Colin Montgomerie**. *The Scot's dour on-course demeanour did not endear him to American spectators, resulting in a number of encounters caused by rogue camera flashes.*

- **John Daly**. *The famously combustible American was fined in 2008 after smashing a fan's camera during the Australian Open in Sydney.*

HOW TO MAKE SURE YOU HAVE FUN!

Don't hurry. Don't worry. You're only here for a short visit. So don't forget to stop and smell the roses.
Walter Hagen

If you get frustrated playing golf, try and remember the reason why it is played so widely in the first place – for fun and relaxation. Dwelling on the bad shots not only means you have less fun, but also disturbs your concentration and harms your overall game.

- **Know the rules**. If you have a good grasp of the rules and etiquette of golf, both you and your companions will get more out of the experience. Similarly, clubs employ strict dress codes for a reason: if you dress like a golfer (see page 27), you are more likely to feel and eventually play like one.

- **Don't get angry!** As important as it may feel, golf is only a game – if you hit a bad shot, take a deep breath and learn from your mistake. If you get tense or angry, your game will suffer.

- **Come prepared**. If you are wearing shorts in the rain, or go out without sunscreen in the midday sun, the round will seem a lot less fun! Also, basic accessories such as a towel to wipe your clubs and an umbrella will improve the quality of your round.

- **Choose your playing partners carefully**. Golf is about socialising and having fun as well as getting the ball in the hole – so don't play with anyone you know whom you will not enjoy playing with. If you don't know anyone who plays golf, you may be able to post a notice at your local course to advertise for the kind of partner you are looking for.

- **Compliment good shots**. It may sound cheesy, but as golf can be enhanced by a positive outlook, vocal encouragement is reward in itself for a shot. It may also make others more willing to do the same to you.

◉ PRACTISING ◉

Success depends on how effectively you manage the game's two ultimate adversaries: the course and yourself.
Jack Nicklaus

Even the best professional golfers never stop practising – Vijay Singh hits golf balls for up to 12 hours a day. Be prepared to change bad habits. This may take patience, especially if you have been playing in the same way for a while, but you will be rewarded for your perseverance in the long term.

DRIVING RANGES

A driving range consists of a large, open space with a line of tees or mats at one end, and is set up for players to practise their swing with no need to worry about where the ball ends up. For a set fee you are given a bucket of 50–100 golf balls (known as 'range balls' because they are cheaper and more durable), which you can hit into the range in your own time. Distance markers and greens, found on most ranges, also allow you to see how far you are hitting and practise your length and accuracy.

How to get the most out of a driving range

- **Warm up before swinging your clubs**. No matter how hard you are planning to hit, you should do some gentle stretching before starting, to avoid pulling any muscles.

- **Take a few practice swings**. This will ensure that your swing is right before you start hitting the balls you paid for.

- **Pick a target to aim at**. Your session will be far more rewarding, and your shots more successful, if you play your shots on the range as you would on the golf course. This also holds true for your pre-shot routine (see page 141).

- **Start with the shorter clubs**. While many amateur golfers are likely to reach straight for the driver, a more sensible approach is to ease your way in by starting with a pitching wedge or sand wedge, which don't require such a large swing. This helps your muscles get into the swing of things, so that by the time you work your way up to the longer clubs, you are fully warmed up and able to swing comfortably.

- **Use all the clubs in your bag**. Try to make sure that you hit a certain number of balls with each of your clubs, rather than just using the driver. Each club requires a slightly different swing and produces a slightly different result, so you need to hone your technique for each of them.

- **Don't just hit the ball as hard as you can**. There is no prize for long-distance hitting on the driving range – the key to improving your swing is to keep a smooth, even tempo.

- **Play to a plan**. You will find your trip to the driving range a lot more productive if you focus on something specific to work on: your swing will suffer if you are trying to think about a combination of factors simultaneously.

There are over 800 driving ranges in the UK. Some can be found next to golf courses or at golf clubs, while others exist as stand-alone facilities. You will be able to find the location of the nearest driving range in the telephone directory, and several websites exist to help you pinpoint the closest facility to you.

Pocket Fact

A normal golf swing utilises up to 32 individual muscles.

PUTTING GREENS

Putting is the most frequently played of all golf strokes – but also the least practised. Luckily, where there is a driving range, there is likely to be a putting green as well. This enables you to practise your short game.

How to get the most out of a putting green

- **Focus on judging distance when you are prastising**. This is the most important factor in successful putting, and also the most controllable. As every green 'breaks' differently, this part of putting improves as your experience of different greens widens.

- **Putt at a variety of different distances**. On a golf course, every putt will be a different length, so it makes sense to prepare for this by practising hitting the ball different distances, rather than trying to go for the hole.

- **If aiming for the hole, practise 'makeable' putts**. For amateurs, this is likely to be around four feet away. Anything further is as likely to stay out as to drop – even professionals don't expect to make every 10-footer they hit.

- **Don't finish with a miss**. Part of the objective of putting practice is to boost your confidence on the green – so finish off with a number of successful putts, no matter how short the distance!

HOW TO GET THE MOST OUT OF PRACTISING

Confidence comes more easily when you are happy with your game, so make sure that you get a professional to improve your technique (see page 153), and put in the hours you need to improve.

Where to practise

- **On the course**. If a shot goes wrong, stay in the same position and swing again to see if you can establish what went awry and correct it for the next time.

- **At home**. You don't need golf balls to practise your swing: try perfecting your stance and grip in a mirror.

- **In the garden**. Try swinging your clubs at dandelions in the garden – you get to practise your swing and do the gardening at the same time!

- **In the bathroom**. A putting machine is available featuring a green in the style of a toilet mat, so you don't have to lose a minute's practice . . .

Pocket Caddie

When you go to a professional tournament, watch the players practising on the driving range and putting green — it's a great way to view all the leading players hitting all kinds of different shots at close quarters.

◉ JUDGING A HOLE ◉

DISTANCE

An ability to judge distance is one of the most important skills on the golf course. For this reason, golf-course designers often design holes to mislead the unwary, with undulating terrain and a minimum of trees.

Tips on judging distance

Here are some of the easiest ways to make sure that you judge distance accurately:

- **Use a caddie (see Chapter 3)**. Caddies are paid to know every detail of the course they are working on. They should be able to tell you the distance to the front of the green, the back of the green, and the pin position, wherever you are on the hole.
- **Use markers on the course**. Distance markers found on sprinkler heads or stakes can be critical in helping you gauge your position and distance from the hole.
- **Use a course-yardage chart**. If you don't have a caddie, a course planner or yardage chart is a useful way to identify your position on the course, and therefore your distance from the hole.
- **Use a GPS 'caddie'** These are a relatively high-tech and expensive way of gauging distance, but are highly reliable and will work from any position.

WHICH CLUB TO USE

It's important to choose the right club for the shot you want to play: this is a combination of the distance you want the ball to travel and the desired loft of the shot. Here are some tips to help you understand which club to use:

1. On the driving range or similar area, hit as many balls with each of your clubs as necessary to understand your average distance with each, with a normal swing. This will help you gauge which club you will need to achieve the distance you require.

2. Understand what kind of loft you want to hit on the shot. For example, if there are bunkers in the way, you would need the shot to carry over them, whereas an unobstructed shot to the green may be played as a 'bump and run' closer to the ground.

PLAYING IN THE WIND

One element that cannot be judged by a GPS or scorecard is the wind. However, by following these simple hints you will be able to give yourself an advantage:

1. Judge wind direction by looking at treetops. The wind can blow in different directions at different heights; so if you are just looking up at the clouds you may misread the true direction.

2. Look at the changes in terrain – if there is a different elevation there may be an updraught.

3. As a rule, the best way to play in any kind of windy conditions is to employ lower, controlled shots with less spin.

Different types of wind

- **Crosswind (wind blowing across the hole)**. Crosswinds pose two key problems: they reduce the distance of your shot, and aggravate any spin on the ball – which means that if you hook or slice the ball it will fly further off course than normal.

- **Headwind (wind blowing towards you)**. If there is a headwind, you need to allow for less distance than normal. The ball will be less affected by a headwind if you keep it low: use a slower swing with less follow-through, keeping your hands in front of the ball up until impact.

- **Tailwind (wind blowing from behind you)**. Hitting with a tailwind, you need to allow for more distance than normal, both in flight and when the ball lands.

◉ HOW TO . . . ◉

GET OUT OF A BUNKER

Golf professionals regard bunker shots as easier than many others – so why do amateurs find them so difficult? A few simple tips can make life in the bunker a lot more straightforward.

Greenside bunkers

1. Make sure you are well dug into the sand for a stable position, and keep your body still throughout the shot.

2. Open both your stance and the club-face – a right-hander should be facing slightly to the left with the club-face directed slightly to the right of where you want to hit it. This enhances the loft of the club-face.

3. Swing the club back until your hands are around shoulder-height, and hit into the sand, slicing across the ball.

4. Aim to impact the sand behind the ball, so your shot brings up sand as well as ball. If you want the ball to run on once it lands, hit around two or three inches behind the ball; for backspin, reduce your impact point to one inch behind the ball.

5. Accelerate through your shot, and follow the ball with your arms and body as the ball emerges from the bunker.

6. Know your limitations – prioritise getting the ball out of the bunker even if that means not aiming directly for the hole every time.

Fairway bunkers

1. Take one club longer than if you were on the fairway, making sure that it has enough loft to clear the bunker.

2. Grip an inch further down the club-shaft.

3. Stand taller than if you are playing from a greenside bunker, as you don't want to hit the sand from a fairway bunker.

4. Use a 'three-quarter'-length swing, slower than your normal speed, in order to lift the ball off the sand.

5. Adjust the length of your follow-through to govern the distance you want your shot to travel.

GET OUT OF THE ROUGH

Not even the best golfers are able to stay on the fairway 100% of the time. Being able to extricate yourself from the rough is one of the most important skills to develop. Keep the following tips in mind:

1. First and foremost, play to get out of the rough! The temptation is always to get the ball as far as possible, but focus on getting back onto the fairway. Take a more lofted club than you would ideally want, to make sure that you get it airborne.

2. Use a 'three-quarter'-length swing, with more acceleration on the downswing than normal, especially if you are caught up in thick rough.

3. Keep a firm grip throughout the shot, to avoid the club-face getting tangled in the undergrowth.

4. Follow through by shifting the weight onto your front foot and turning your hips, even after the ball has gone.

Pocket Caddie

Whether in a bunker or the rough, don't go for a 'glory shot' that you have minimal chance of making. Play within your capabilities and your overall score will usually be lower.

PUTT

Putting is the single biggest differentiating factor between a good round and a great round. The secret of great putting is not just being able to hole long putts – not even the professionals can do that every time – but also being able to judge the right pace of a putt to leave it as near to the hole as possible. There are several short cuts to developing a reliable putting game:

1. When trying to read the line of a putt, always look from behind the hole as well as from the ball to the hole.

2. Hold the putter with a light grip – this will enable you to feel the weight of the putter's head in order to better judge the distance.

3. Stand with your eyes directly over the ball.

4. Position the face of the putter square to the target line, and keep square to the line when you swing.

5. Putt with your arms, not with your wrists: the putting stroke should look like a pendulum swinging in a grandfather clock. Your head and body should also be still, with your arms doing all the work.

6. Keep the speed and rhythm of your forward swing the same as your back swing – avoid any change in the speed of your stroke.

7. Strike the ball in the centre of the putter. Keep your head down all the way through the stroke – don't look up straight-away to follow the ball's path.

Pocket Caddie 🖊
To help you keep your head steady, try counting to two after putting before you look up to see where the ball has gone.

DRIVE

> *The golf swing is like a suitcase into which we are trying to pack one too many things.*
> John Updike

To be a good golfer you have to have a reliable swing, enabling you to be great from tee to green. This is one thing the world's top golfers all have in common, with green play and mental strength separating the very best players from the rest.

What are the basics of a consistent swing?

- Develop a grip that feels right for you. While there is no single recommended gripping style, here are the three most common:

  - **Overlapping grip** (also known as the Vardon Overlap). The little finger of the bottom hand on the club is placed between the index and middle fingers of the top hand. This grip tends to be most common among golf professionals.

  - **Interlocking grip**. The little finger of the bottom hand on the club interlocks with the index finger of the top hand. This grip is often preferred by people with small hands, and by beginners.

  - **Ten-finger grip** (also known as the Baseball Grip). The little finger of the bottom hand on the club rests against the index finger of the top hand, but there is no overlap or interlock. This grip is the simplest for beginners to master.

- Keep the pressure on your grip consistent so the club doesn't slip – but not too tight, otherwise you may lose speed in the swing.

- Stand with your shoulders level and your knees slightly flexed.

- Swing back the club in as compact a movement as possible, keeping your wrist position the same throughout the motion. Maintain a consistent spine angle all the way through the swing.

- It doesn't make a difference whether your swing is fast or slow: the main thing is that you keep a consistent rhythm throughout the swing.

- At the top of your back swing, try and make your forearms form the top two sides of a level 'triangle', with the shaft of the club pointing towards the target line.

- Strike through the ball, rather than just at it. In other words, make sure that your club-head follows through even after impact.

- When hitting with an iron from the fairway, you need to hit down in order for the ball to go up. If you hit down too steeply you will lose control of the spin and trajectory of your shot. Use the size of the divot your club takes out of the ground to gauge whether you are hitting down too steeply: the divot should be long and thin rather than large or deep.

◉ LESSONS AND PROS ◉

Golf, like measles, should be caught young.
P.G. Wodehouse

Why have golfing lessons?

- A lesson with a professional golf instructor is the best possible introduction to playing golf, ideally before you even take your first tee shot.

- You will be more likely to improve quickly if you are taught the correct technique from the start – if you delay having lessons it can be a longer and more expensive process to change any bad habits you have developed.

How to arrange lessons and get the most out of them

- Contact your local golf club or driving range for more information.

- Whether your lesson takes place as part of a group, or one-on-one with a golfing professional, will depend upon your budget and learning preference. Ask around a few different places before booking, to make sure you get the option that suits you best.

8

SOME FUN FOR THE 19TH HOLE: GOLF TRIVIA

◉ GOLF ON FILM ◉

Golf has provided a rich seam for film-makers over the years, from true tales of personal triumph to extreme comedies. The tournament format of four 18-hole rounds often provides a natural framework for drama.

Three Little Beers

Released: 1935

Starred: The Three Stooges

Tagline: 'Some foam, eh, kid?'

About the film: Slapstick comedy with The Three Stooges as bumbling brewery workers who sneak onto a golf course to get in some pre-tournament practice. Mayhem ensues . . .

Verdict: 7/10. One of the Stooges' finest short films.

Follow the Sun

Released: 1951

Starred: Glenn Ford, Anne Baxter

Guest star: Sam Snead

Tagline: 'The real-life love story of two kids from Texas.'

About the film: Reverential biopic of Ben Hogan's legendary career (see page 87), which was rife with dramatic potential. From his pre-war days as a poverty-stricken professional, to his service in the military during the Second World War, it culminates in the near-fatal road accident and follows his unexpected professional and public renaissance. Hogan's life story seemed to be made for Hollywood.

Verdict: 6/10.

Pocket Fact ⚑

Part of the film was shot on location at Pebble Beach.

Pat & Mike

Released: 1952

Starred: Spencer Tracy, Katharine Hepburn

Guest star: Babe Zaharias

Tagline: 'Together again – and it's no fib, their funniest hit since *Adam's Rib*.'

About the film: Romantic comedy starring Hepburn as a female golfer who initially despises her shady manager, only to eventually become attracted to him. The golf scenes play second fiddle to the exchanges between the two leads, who worked so well together that this was one of nine films in which they featured as a pair.

Verdict: 7/10. Called 'One of the season's gayest comedies' by *Time* magazine, the film was reputedly Hepburn's favourite of those she and Tracy starred in.

Pocket Fact ⚑

Hepburn, a capable golfer, played all her own golf shots in the film.

The Caddy

Released: 1953

Starred: Dean Martin, Jerry Lewis

Guest stars: Ben Hogan, Sam Snead, Byron Nelson

Tagline: 'Goofy Golfers . . . winning the laughing cup!'

About the film: 'Odd couple'-style comedy featuring Lewis as caddie to Dean Martin. After causing a commotion and being disqualified from a tournament, they are offered a job in show business.

Verdict: 5/10.

Pocket Fact

The film featured Martin's first rendition of That's Amore, *which became one of his signature songs.*

Caddyshack
Released: 1980

Starred: Chevy Chase, Bill Murray

Tagline: 'The snobs against the slobs.'

About the film: Endlessly quotable cult comedy. An exclusive golf club struggles to deal with the plans of a real-estate developer and a destructive gopher, while the working-class caddies wreak havoc on the fairways.

Quotable quote: 'Two wrongs don't make a right, but three rights make a left.'

Verdict: 8/10. Irreverent: hit-and-miss but also very funny.

Pocket Fact

Bill Murray, writer Brian Doyle-Murray and director Harold Ramis had all worked as caddies as teenagers.

Dead Solid Perfect
Released: 1988

Starred: Randy Quaid, Kathryn Harrold, Corinne Bohrer

Guest star: Peter Jacobsen

Tagline: 'Based on the funniest and bawdiest golf novel ever!'

About the film: 'Warts and all' film charting life on the road for a run-of-the-mill touring professional, based on an original novel by Dan Jenkins.

Verdict: 7/10. Underrated film made for cable TV.

Pocket Fact 🏌

Jenkins made an un-credited cameo as a hotel guest.

Happy Gilmore
Released: 1996

Starred: Adam Sandler

Guest star: Lee Trevino

Tagline: 'He doesn't play golf . . . he destroys it.'

About the film: Goofy comedy with Sandler as an ice-hockey player, who finds far more success on the golf course than on the ice rink, after originally entering golf tournaments to raise money for his grandmother.

Quotable quote: 'It's all in the hips. It's all in the hips. It's all in the hips. It's all in the hips.'

Verdict: 6/10. Enjoyable enough fare for golf buffs, if you disengage your brain.

Pocket Fact 🏌

The 'Happy Gilmore swing', taking a running swing at the ball, has been found by a Canadian judge to 'breach a duty of care' — which means that anyone trying it leaves themselves open to civil liability if things go wrong.

Tin Cup

Released: 1996

Starred: Kevin Costner, Rene Russo

Guest star: Johnny Miller

Tagline: 'Golf pro. Love amateur.'

About the film: Fading golfer, Roy McAvoy (Costner), battles to qualify for the US Open to win the heart of his psychiatrist (Russo), who is the girlfriend of his main rival, played by Don Johnson.

Verdict: 7/10. The film wins points for avoiding the obvious ending. 'Works for viewers of any handicap,' wrote the *Washington Post*.

𝒫ocket 𝒻act ⚑

The lake, which plays a pivotal role in the film, was built by the film company at Tubac Golf Resort, Arizona, and remains there to this day.

The Legend of Bagger Vance

Released: 2000

Starred: Will Smith, Matt Damon, Charlize Theron

Tagline: 'Some things can't be learned. They must be remembered.'

About the film: Earnest tale of self-discovery set in 1931. A 'down on his luck' golfer turns both his game and his life around by taking the advice of a mysterious caddie, enabling him to take on Bobby Jones and Walter Hagen in an exhibition match.

Quotable quote: 'And now I'm supposed to run into your arms and melt like butter on a hot muffin?'

Verdict: 6/10. 'A lightweight, modestly engaging yarn,' wrote *Variety*.

Pocket Fact 🚩

The name of Bagger Vance (the caddie) is derived from Bhagavan, the name used by the Hindu god, Krishna; R. Juna (the golfer) is derived from Arjuna, the prince who absorbed Krishna's teachings in the original Hindu text.

Bobby Jones – Stroke of Genius

Released: 2004

Starred: James Caviezel, Claire Forlani

Tagline: 'There are finer things than winning championships.'

About the film: Earnest biopic of Bobby Jones, who won all four major championships before retiring at just 28, and who founded the US Masters.

Verdict: 5/10. Manages to make Jones' incredible career seem less exciting than it was.

Pocket Fact 🚩

The film was the first-ever permitted to film on location at St Andrews.

The Greatest Game Ever Played

Released: 2005

Starred: Shia LaBeouf, Stephen Dillane

Tagline: 'Everything begins with a dream.'

About the film: Dramatisation of the 1913 US Open, where local unknown, Francis Ouimet, beats the British legends, Harry Vardon and Ted Ray, to become the tournament's first amateur champion (see page 98).

Quotable quote: 'Read it, roll it, hole it.'

Verdict: 7/10. The story of the tournament was made for melodrama. 'A well-crafted entertainment,' wrote *Empire*.

◉ GOLF ON TV ◉

The Open Championship is on the list of 'crown jewels' in the British sporting calendar: these are events that are required by law to be shown on terrestrial TV, because of their level of national importance. Other 'crown jewels' include the FA Cup Final, the Wimbledon tennis championships, and the Grand National. The Open is currently on the 'B-list', which requires at a minimum that highlights are shown on terrestrial TV, although this is currently under discussion.

Most golf tournaments are televised on satellite TV, with terrestrial TV covering a smaller selection of high-profile tournaments. In 2010, tournaments covered on terrestrial TV included the following:

- The Open (BBC)
- US Masters (BBC)
- European PGA Championship (BBC)
- Women's British Open (BBC)

Pocket Fact 🏌

A celebrity golf tournament called The All Star Cup *was screened on Sky in 2005–2006 after ITV turned down the show. The teams included Michael Douglas and Catherine Zeta Jones representing Team USA and Team Europe respectively.*

◉ GOLF ON THE BOOKSHELF ◉

Whether due to the beauty of its surroundings, the legends and stories that it has created, or the time it affords for contemplation, golf has a longer and nobler literary history than most sports. Here is the cream of the crop, from the earliest instruction books to the exhaustively researched biographies of the present day.

INSTRUCTION BOOKS

Ever since the first of its kind appeared in 1857, instruction books have formed the major genre of golf literature. The first truly memorable titles appeared after golf's first popularity boom in the 1920s. Some have aged as times changed, but a handful of landmark publications are still invaluable today, despite the many hundreds of similar books packing the shelves.

- **Bobby Jones – *On Golf* (1930)**. One of the earliest and best golf instruction books, Jones' advice is communicated in accessible prose, and has recently formed the basis of video based tips on The Golf Channel.

- **Tommy Armour – *How To Play Your Best Golf All The Time* (1953)**. Armour, three times a major champion, set out his instructions clearly and methodically to become one of golf's great teachers.

- **Ben Hogan with Herbert Warren Wind – *Five Lessons: The Modern Fundamentals of Golf* (1957)**. Hogan's golf swing is the stuff of legend, and in this book he tells you in typically concise fashion how it can be done, complete with superb line drawings of Hogan by Anthony Ravielli.

- **Jack Nicklaus with Ken Bowden – *Golf My Way* (1974)**. Nicklaus examines each shot in his repertoire in detail. His golf swing was very distinctive and not for everyone, but every page lends fascinating insight into Nicklaus' greatness. Recreating major shots from his career and also analysing his rivals' playing styles, Nicklaus' instruction book is one of the most enjoyable.

- **David Leadbetter – *The Golf Swing* (1990)**. Leadbetter's first book is still the complete reference book for anyone looking for advice on their swing.

- **Harvey Penick – *Harvey Penick's Little Red Book* (1992)**. The book was compiled from Penick's jottings on scraps of paper, accumulated over 60 years of golf teaching. Simple and effective guidance from the man who taught Ben Crenshaw and Tom Kite.

- **Dr. Bob Rotella with Bob Cullen** – *Golf Is Not a Game of Perfect* **(1995)**. The influential sports psychologist delivers advice on gaining and maintaining confidence and concentration.

- **Fred Shoemaker** – *Extraordinary Golf* **(1996)**. Shoemaker advances his strategies, enabling golfers to focus on every aspect of their game. Short on technical tips and long on the benefits of focusing on the experience, rather than on the outcome.

- **Tiger Woods** – *How I Play Golf* **(2001)**. Although the focus is on the basic fundamentals of the game, there are enough hints and pointers to interest even lower handicappers.

AUTOBIOGRAPHIES AND BIOGRAPHIES

As in all other sports, the stories of golf are constantly retold, although not always in the words of those who created them. A recent sub-genre, pioneered by George Plimpton in the 1960s, is 'participatory journalism', where the author relates his own experiences.

- **Robert T. Jones Jr and O.B. Keeler** – *Down The Fairway* **(1927)**. Bobby Jones showed the same nerve in writing his life story at 24 as he did in winning a succession of major championships. The wit and wisdom he imparts makes the end result fully worthwhile: 'I never learnt anything from a match that I won.'

- **George Plimpton** – *The Bogey Man* **(1968)**. The basic premise of the book is to describe the month Plimpton spent playing in pro-am tournaments on the PGA Tour, but this is only part of the appeal of a book enhanced by some wonderful insights and stories from the leading professionals.

- **Jack Nicklaus with Herbert Warren Wind** – *The Greatest Game Of All* **(1969)**. Although not yet even halfway through his catalogue of major triumphs, this recounting makes compelling reading; revealing not only Nicklaus' golfing intelligence but also other aspects of his life so far.

- **David Owen** – *My Usual Game* **(1995)**. Owen, who has written for *Golf Digest* and the *New Yorker*, brings a sharp and irreverent slant to the game as he recounts his reintroduction to golf.

- **Curt Sampson – *Hogan* (1996)**. A fascinating account of the forces that shaped the life of one of golf's greatest and most secretive players.

- **Mark Frost – *The Greatest Game Ever Played* (2004)**. Focusing on the amazing story of Francis Ouimet at the 1913 US Open, Frost masterfully juxtaposes the underdog with Harry Vardon, the six-times British Open champion, who started as overwhelming favourite.

- **Tom Coyne – *Paper Tiger* (2006)**. Coyne devotes a whole year to playing golf, just to see if he can improve enough to reach a professional standard. He doesn't, but all is not lost as the result is this entertaining diversion.

FICTION

Aside from the immortal Wodehouse stories, golf has not been frequently mythologised in literary fiction – maybe because many true-life stories are better than fiction!

- **P.G. Wodehouse – *The Golf Omnibus* (1973)**. As a frequent chronicler of the English upper classes, it was perhaps inevitable that Wodehouse would touch upon the game they (and he) loved. His golf stories effortlessly combine the toils of various star-crossed lovers, familiar to Wodehouse buffs, with the intricacies of Golden-Age golf, watched over benevolently by the club's 'Oldest Member'.

- **Dan Jenkins – *Dead Solid Perfect* (1974)**. Jenkins, who was an amateur golfer himself before turning his hand to writing humorously about it instead, produced one of the most entertaining evocations of the game in history.

- **Steven Pressfield – *The Legend of Bagger Vance: A Novel of Golf and the Game of Life* (1995)**. The story of a meeting between Bobby Jones, Walter Hagen, and an amateur golfer with a mysterious caddie makes for an intriguing and enjoyable novel. Critics prefer the book to the film.

- **John Updike – *Golf Dreams* (1996)**. Updike is known as the poet of golf, for his lyrical descriptions of the game and its trappings. This collection of essays is possibly his best.

- **Rick Reilly – *Missing Links* (1996)**. Reilly, who writes for *Sports Illustrated*, made his debut as a novelist with the story of four no-hopers who play at the worst course in the USA, and accept a bet to play at the elite club next door.

MAGAZINES

A range of periodicals exists to give you a regular fix of golf reading. Here are those you are most likely to find on the shelf:

- ***Today's Golfer***. One of Britain's leading, monthly golf magazines. Good for advice on new kit and tips to improve technique – making it particularly useful for beginners.

- ***Golf World***. First published in 1947, this glossy, weekly publication is the oldest golf magazine in the USA. It is particularly useful for course reviews, tournament coverage, and articles on major stars.

- ***Golf International***. This monthly publication also contains elements of a men's-lifestyle magazine, with tournament updates and golf instruction alongside car reviews and property tips.

- ***Women and Golf***. Monthly magazine aimed at women, with updates on the latest tournaments and equipment.

◉ GOLF ON THE COMPUTER ◉

COMPUTER GAMES

Golf games have been a fundamental part of computer game-play since the days of the Commodore 64 and the Amiga. Today, all the major gaming consoles have at least one golf offering:

- ***Tiger Woods PGA Tour* series** (Playstation, Xbox, Wii, PC). First released in 1998, the franchise leads the playing field, and has been updated nearly every year since. The course simulations are so good that professional players have been known to use the game to get a feel for a new course before they actually play it.

- *Everybody's Golf* (Playstation). Unashamedly fun golf game, although less true to real life than the *Tiger Woods* games. It still boasts superb graphics, but is also accessible and addictive.

- *Nintendo Wii Golf* (part of the Wii Sports bundle). As well as being an accessible way to get the whole family into golf games, the Wii is highly interactive because you actually take a swing – using the controller like a club, in the same way you would on the course. Other golf games available on the Wii include *Tiger Woods PGA Tour* and *We Love Golf!*

- **Online golf games**. There is a huge variety of golf games available online, from mini-golf in exotic locations like Stonehenge and Easter Island, to full-course simulations. Most are free, although some require you to register or download software.

ONLINE GOLF FORUMS

Whether you are looking for guidance on your golf game or a group of friends to talk golf with, a vast number of golf forums exist to cater for your needs.

- The Sand Trap, an online golf-fan site, has a well-visited forum (www.thesandtrap.com/forum) where you can talk about everything golf, from course design to playing tips.

- The website at www.golfwrx.com has an enormous forum (www.forums.golfwrx.com) covering a bewildering variety of topics, from a 'For Sale' forum to an area especially for seniors.

- The Golf-Monthly forum (www.forums.golf-monthly.co.uk) is a UK forum with over 200,000 posts, covering discussion of all aspects of the game. It includes an opportunity to 'ask the experts', and arrange games with like-minded readers.

◉ GOLF QUIZ ◉

See if you can answer these questions about golf. All of the answers can be found on page 178

1. Which course hosts the US Masters?

2. Which golfer has won the most major championships?

3. How many golf clubs are you allowed in total?

4. What did Sandy Lyle select as main course for the Masters Club Dinner, held to mark his US Masters triumph?

5. What is the name given to the type of course that hosts the Open Championship?

6. Which golfer is one of only three people to have their image on a British banknote in their own lifetime?

7. Why was the first Open Championship trophy, the Championship Belt, replaced by the Claret Jug?

8. In which discipline did female golfer Babe Zaharias win two Olympic gold medals?

9. King James II of Scotland banned golf because it was distracting his subjects from which pastime?

10. In which country is the world's longest golf course?

11. Which is the lower score: an albatross or a condor?

12. Who hit the longest successful televised putt in a competitive tournament?

13. Which world record did Arnold Palmer set in 1976?

14. Which rising star won the US Amateur Championship an unprecedented three consecutive years from 1994–1996?

15. Whose last words were: 'That was a great game of golf, fellas!'?

9

BIRDIE OR BOGEY? GLOSSARY OF GOLF TERMS

Over the years, golf has developed a language all of its own, which you will need to understand when out on the course or watching the game on TV. This chapter covers the basic jargon and explains how the most interesting terms developed.

Abnormal ground condition
Casual water (e.g. a puddle), ground under repair, or holes or mounds made by burrowing animals, reptiles or birds.

Albatross
The name given to a score of three strokes under par for a single hole (e.g. playing a par 5 in two).

How did it get its name? The term is an extension of 'birdie' and 'eagle' (for scores of one and two under par respectively).

Pocket Fact
The most famous albatross was 'the shot heard around the world', made by Gene Sarazen at the 1935 Masters. His second shot, holed from 235 yards at the par-5 15th hole, not only took him into a victorious play-off but also helped raise the profile of the then-fledgling tournament.

Amateur
A golfer who does not earn money from playing.

Approach
A shot aimed at the green from the fairway or rough.

Back nine
The second half of an 18-hole round.

Birdie
Playing a hole in one stroke under par.

How did it get its name? 'Bird' was 19th-century American slang for something excellent. A great shot therefore became known as a 'bird', and 'birdie' was used to designate an under-par score by the turn of the century.

Bite
(Of a golf ball) To stop where it lands.

Bogey
Playing a hole in one stroke over par.

How did it get its name? The Bogey Man was a popular British music-hall song of the 1890s, and the term was coined by golfers as a moniker for the testing, new adversary we now know as 'par', which was being adopted across the land. In the early 20th century, the USA updated their 'par' criteria to compensate for improving scores, but Britain did not follow – this led to Americans referring to one over par as the British 'Bogey' score.

Bunker (USA: Sand-trap)
A crater-like area, usually filled with sand, deemed as a 'hazard'.

Burn
Scottish word for a stream, as in 'Barry Burn', the famous water hazard on the last hole at Carnoustie (see page 52).

Caddie
The golfer's companion, whose primary roles are to carry the clubs and advise on all aspects of the game, particularly club and shot selection.

How did it get its name? The most likely origin is from the French word 'cadet', or 'youngest of the family', which first appeared in English in the 1630s.

Chip

A lofted shot, usually from just off the green, after which the ball rolls across the green towards the hole.

Clubhouse

A building, usually beside the first tee and the last green, where club members can meet and use all the facilities provided.

Pocket Fact

The first golf clubhouse in the world was built at Leith in 1768.

Condor

The name given to a score of four strokes under par for a single hole (e.g. playing a par 5 in one shot).

How did it get its name? The term is an extension of 'albatross' (for a score of three under par).

Pocket Fact

Only four condors have been recorded in golfing history — all holes in one on par-5 holes.

Course

The area on which golf is played.

Cut

The line delineating players retained for the final rounds of a tournament. Those retained are said to have 'made' the cut; those left out have 'missed' it.

Divot

A section of earth uprooted when a shot is played from the fairway. Players must replace any divots they dislodge on their way round the course.

Dog-leg

A hole that turns to the left or right between tee and green, forcing the golfer to play around the corner.

How did it get its name? The term refers to the crooked appearance of a dog's hind leg.

Pocket Fact 📍

A hole that bends twice is called a 'double dog-leg'.

Draw

A shot where the ball is deliberately curved inwards (as opposed to a hook, where the same effect happens accidentally).

Drive

A long-range shot played from the tee.

Driver

A club designed for drives from the tee.

Driving range

A large, open space set up for golfers to practise their drives.

Eagle

Playing a hole in two strokes under par.

How did it get its name? The term is an extension of 'birdie' (for a score of one under par).

Etiquette

An important part of the rules of golf, governing behaviour on the course.

Fade

A shot where the ball is deliberately curved outwards (as opposed to a slice, where the same effect happens accidentally).

Fairway

The area of mown grass between the tee and the green.

Fore

A cry to warn other players or spectators of an approaching ball.

How did it get its name? The most likely explanation is that the warning was originally shouted in the late 19th century to alert forecaddies (whose job it was to find the landing position of the players' golf balls) that a shot was heading their way. Over time, the shout of 'Forecaddie!' became shortened to 'Fore!'

Four-ball

A competition between two pairs of golfers, each hitting their own ball. In match play, four-ball is decided by the lowest score on each hole.

Foursomes

A competition between two pairs of golfers, with each pair hitting alternate shots of the same ball.

Front nine

The first half of an 18-hole round.

Grand slam

Winning all four major championships in the same season.

Green

An area of very short grass within which the hole is located.

Ground under repair

An area of the course that is damaged or under repair.

Handicap

The number of shots above par a player expects to shoot. Golfers should constantly maintain their handicaps, in order to be able to compete fairly with other players.

Hazard

An obstacle on the course, usually applied to bunkers or water.

Hole

1. The sunken hollow in the green into which the ball must be hit.

2. The entire playing area from the tee to the green. A championship golf course consists of 18 holes.

Pocket Fact ⛳
The hole must be 4¼ inches (108mm) in diameter.

Hole in one (USA: ace)
Getting the ball into the hole with your first shot from the tee.

Pocket Fact ⛳
The oldest player to hit a hole in one on a regulation golf course was 102-year-old Elsie McLean. 'For an old lady,' she said, 'I still hit the ball pretty good.'

Honour
The right to play first off the tee. Often determined by the toss of a coin on the first hole, and subsequently given to the player who won the previous hole.

Hook
A shot inadvertently skewed to the left for a right-hander, and to the right for a left-hander.

Immovable obstruction
A man-made obstruction: e.g. temporary car park, roadworks, building.

Iron
A club with a metal head, used to hit the ball long distances. Irons are numbered from 1–9: the numbers increase with the loft of the club-face.

Links
Areas of coastal wasteland – often sand dunes covered with grass – on which the first golf courses were built. The term is now applied to golf courses that demonstrate these characteristics.

How did it get its name? From the Anglo-Saxon word 'hlinc', which originally meant 'ridge', but came to be applied to the type of coastal wasteland between sea and land on which golf was first played.

Loft (for clubs)

The angle at which the club-face deviates from the shaft. Increased loft enables a shot to be propelled higher into the air at the expense of distance.

Match play

A competitive format where the competition is decided on a hole-by-hole basis, with the best score on each hole winning the hole. The winner is the player or team to win the most holes.

Mulligan

A retaken shot, most often after a miss from the tee.

How did it get its name? The origin of the term, which was in widespread use by the 1940s, is uncertain. There are three potential explanations – which do you find more believable?

- Mr David Mulligan, a prominent Canadian businessman who owned and managed several hotels in America, mishit a tee shot at his country club and quickly took a second attempt, calling it a 'correction shot' to the chagrin of his companions, who renamed the practice a 'mulligan'.

- Earlier in the 20th century, American saloons would place a free bottle of liquor on the bar for customers to help themselves. The name of this free bottle? A Mulligan.

- In the early 20th century Irish-Americans began to join American golf clubs and were looked down upon for lowering the standards of golf. This, a 'Mulligan', is a by word for golfing incompetence.

Nearest point of relief

The closest point at which the golfer can play with an unobstructed line to the hole. May be invoked in response to an immovable obstruction.

Out of bounds

Area designated as beyond the boundaries of the hole.

Par

The amount of shots a scratch golfer should take to complete a hole. Most holes are classified as par 3, 4 or 5, with distance being the primary differentiating factor.

Penalty

The punishment for any breach of the rules. Penalties can vary from additional strokes and monetary fines, to disqualification, depending on the offence.

Pin

A pole, usually with a flag attached to the top, inserted into the hole to show golfers playing their approach shots where the hole is.

Pitch

A lofted shot, usually played as an approach shot to the green.

Plus fours

Fashionable inter-war golfing attire, consisting of baggy knicker-bockers that the golfer tucked into long socks. Recently popularised for a modern audience by the late Payne Stewart.

How did it get its name? The 'plus four' refers to the number of inches longer below the knee that the trousers were than standard knickerbockers. This extra length gave them the baggy appearance when tucked into socks.

Pro-am

A match or tournament combining professional and amateur players on the same team.

Putt

Shot made on the green, where the ball is rolled towards the hole.

How did it get its name? As a variation of the word 'put', similar to 'shot putting'.

Putter

A square-faced club specifically designed for use on the putting green.

Round

A full circuit of the golf course, with each hole played consecutively. On most courses a round consists of 18 holes.

Rough

Longer grass or unchecked foliage bordering the fairway or green.

Scratch

A handicap of zero: i.e. professional standard.

Short game

The shots you play around the green: e.g. pitching, chipping and putting.

Slice

A shot inadvertently skewed to the right for a right-hander, and to the left for a left-hander.

Stroke

To bring the club forward with the intention of striking the ball. The term is also used in reference to the number of shots that a player has taken (or is deemed, by penalty, to have taken).

Stroke-and-distance

Incurring an extra shot, then having to play from the same position as your previous shot. The player can do this at any time, if this is the best option given the position of the original shot.

Stroke play

A competitive format, used in all major professional tournaments, where the competition is decided by the total number of strokes taken by each player.

Swing

The movement of hitting the ball, usually with woods or irons.

Tee

The designated area from which the first shot is played on each hole. Many courses have several different tees, which enable the hole to be played at varying lengths, ensuring that it is playable for all golfers.

How did it get its name? From the Gaelic word 'tigh', or 'house'. In the sport of curling, this was related to the circles on the rink, and similarly the original golf tees were within a circle of one club's length from the hole.

Top

To hit the upper half of the ball, resulting in a shot along the ground with no loft.

Tour

An organised schedule of individual, professional golf tournaments.

Water hazard

Predominantly lakes, ponds or streams found on the course.

Pocket Fact

It is not actually necessary for a water hazard to contain water! If a water hazard is dry when your ball lands in it, it is played under the same rules.

Wedge

A special type of iron club with an extremely lofted face. Different types of wedges exist for pitching or getting out of bunkers.

Woods

Traditionally wooden-headed clubs (now made of metal) which are used for hitting long shots off the tee (the driver) or from the fairway (fairway woods). Like irons, woods are numbered in accordance with the increasing loft of the club.

Answers

1. Augusta National in Georgia, USA, hosts the US Masters.
2. Jack Nicklaus, who has won 18 majors.
3. You are allowed a maximum of 14 clubs.
4. The 1988 winner, proud Scotsman Sandy chose haggis as the Masters Club Dinner.
5. The Open Championship is always held on a links course. See page 42 for the definition of a links course.
6. Jack Nicklaus appeared on a commemorative £5 produced by the Bank of Scotland to mark his farewell appearance at the Old Course.
7. The rules of the Open Championship stated that anyone who won the title three consecutive times got to keep the prize, the Championship Belt. When Young Tom Morris won the Championship three times in a row the committee was forced to find a new prize, the Claret Jug, which now remains the property of the committee.
8. Babe Zaharias won two gold medals in track and field at the 1932 Olympics.
9. King James II banned golf because it was distracting his subjects from their archery practice.
10. Nullarbor Links, the longest course in the world, is in Australia.
11. A condor is the lower score. It is four strokes under par, while an albatross is three strokes under par.
12. Terry Wogan hit a 33-yard putt at Gleneagles in 1981.
13. In 1976 Arnold Palmer flew around the world in 57 hours, 25 minutes and 42 seconds, setting a new world record for circumnavigating the globe.
14. Tiger Woods won the US Amateur Championship three times between 1994 and 1996.
15. Bing Crosby's last words were: 'That was a great game of golf, fellas!' before he died in 1978.